PHENOMENAL
TEAMS

Phenomenal Teams: How leaders build high-performance teams that last

Published by Grammar Factory Publishing, an imprint of MacMillan Company Limited.

Grammar Factory Publishing
MacMillan Company Limited
25 Telegram Mews, 39th Floor, Suite 3906
Toronto, Ontario, Canada
M5V 3Z1

www.grammarfactory.com

Dooley, Garie
      Phenomenal Teams: How leaders build high-performance teams that last / Garie Dooley.

Paperback ISBN 978-1-989737-16-3
eBook ISBN 978-1-989737-17-0

1. BUS071000 BUSINESS & ECONOMICS / Leadership. 2. BUS041000 BUSINESS & ECONOMICS / Management. 3. BUS030000 BUSINESS & ECONOMICS / Human Resources & Personnel Management.

Production Credits
Cover design by Julia Kuris
Interior layout design by Dania Zafar
Book production and editorial services by Grammar Factory Publishing

PHENOMENAL TEAMS

HOW LEADERS BUILD HIGH-PERFORMANCE TEAMS THAT LAST

GARIE DOOLEY

"The art of winning, whether it be in sport or in business, has often been likened to strategy in chess. The beautiful outcome when building a Phenomenal Team is that every piece has the capability of a King - every piece, no matter where they are on the board, has the capability to Lead."

GARIE DOOLEY

ABOUT THE AUTHOR

Garie Dooley is obsessed with stretching and growing 'the brave', the 'mavericks in the making', and 'the game changers' to create Phenomenal Teams and Legendary Leaders.

As a speaker, coach, facilitator, and now author, Garie has developed a unique, powerful, practical, and facilitated framework that enables teams to safely stretch, grow, and consistently deliver industry-leading performance. He has applied this in a broad range of settings, from elite sports teams and small- to medium-sized businesses through to national and multinational organisations.

Very few consultants in the country can lay claim to the breadth of success Garie has had. He has supported teams from corporate Australia as well as elite sport, including AFL Premiership winners, Super Rugby League Championship winners, Sheffield Shield winners, netball grand finalists, and Rugby League State of Origin winners.

Garie has held senior corporate roles such as marketing manager, retail manager, regional director, sales manager and CEO at state, national, and regional levels in organisations across a number of environments, including sport, telecommunications, recruitment, franchising, and consulting.

It is this breadth of experience that serves to enhance his credibility when it comes to the building of Phenomenal Teams.

Garie's framework is real, practical, and relevant, borne out of the cumulative experience gained through these roles. In fact, by his own admission, what really gives him credibility is the fact that he has made all the mistakes mentioned in this book!

Which is why your next step is to read it and action the ideas contained within its pages, so you don't make those same mistakes.

Ready?

GARIEDOOLEY.COM

ACKNOWLEDGEMENTS

So many people ... so little space!

There have been so many people across so many different aspects of my life who have shaped this book.

Whether teachers and students I knew when I was working in education, or players, opponents and coaches from my days playing football in the National Soccer League, or managers and leaders in my corporate life, or fellow consultants, facilitators and clients in my consulting life – all had an impact.

And to all of the pioneers who have gone before me, who have built models and frameworks for the development of teams and leadership, and who have been brave in challenging mindsets around performance, you have had an impact as well. Thank you so much for sharing.

And to my family ... without your love, guidance, and support, I am just that obsessive, passionate bloke who loves teams!

Finally, I want to thank you — the reader. You are an inspiration, you are a maverick, and you could become that game changer who is always talked about. Read on and stay brave!

It is important to appreciate that sustained organisational success – success that con-sistently exceeds expectations – is not just about talent. Whether it be in business or sport, this success is driven by Phenomenal Teams, led by Legendary Leaders.

CONTENTS

INTRODUCTION

Have you ever watched your team at work and struggled with how you could possibly ask them to give more or work any harder after what has already been a gruelling and challenging period?

How often have you taken a step back, looked at your team, and wondered if you will ever get this group of highly talented and competitive people to accept different roles and possibly sacrifice their own prominence for the greater good? Or how they can possibly deliver more with less?

Or grappled with why you are not consistently overachieving and overdelivering, given the available talent?

Or even just sensed that something isn't quite right in your team, that you are not really enjoying things at the moment, and wondered if any of the team feel the same?

Well, if you *have* experienced these concerns (or similar ones) with regard to the growth and development of your team, you are not alone.

Steve Kerr, a well-known team builder in sport, the 2016 NBA Coach of the Year, and head coach of the championship-winning Golden State Warriors, probably speaks for us all when he suggests that building consistently high-performing, selfless teams is really hard work. Which is why it isn't done very often.

If it is so hard, why bother focusing and spending time on building great teams? Why not just get the team to work harder to hit the new plan, even if we have to rely on the same people (some of whom are disruptive) to do it?

Well, to at least get us thinking deeply about why we should be investing in the development of our teams, let's look at what the research tells us.

According to a 2013 study of over 2,200 participants by Booz and Company, eighty-four per cent of respondents believed that team culture was critical to their success.

Now, let's match that with data from Gallup suggesting that highly engaged teams have the potential to deliver nineteen per cent more income and twenty-eight per cent more in earnings growth than teams with low levels of engagement.

Imagine how you and your team would be described and how you would feel if you were able to consistently deliver twenty per cent growth on whatever your team's key deliverable is?

But let's also look at some of the challenges.

A recent study of 118 organisations conducted by the Centre for Creative Leadership found that:

- only fifty-three per cent of teams were consistently exceeding the organisation's expectations;
- thirty-six per cent of teams do not bring conflict to the surface and resolve it effectively; and
- thirty per cent of team members did not enjoy being in their respective team.

And the impact of these findings?

Gallup observed that

- poorly managed teams are, on average, fifty per cent less productive and forty-four per cent less profitable than well-managed teams.

Forbes identified that

- collaborative environments were *five times* more likely to be high performing.

And from my own experience:

- Discretionary effort – the effort team members give when they don't have to – is a direct result of being *truly* engaged.

> *It is concerning that, in a number of environments, leaders have clearly lost sight of the fact that people love being in teams – and they REALLY love being in successful teams.*

Having team members who feel highly engaged is the key to your team's ongoing success, because just being in the team isn't enough.

PwC highlighted this point when they estimated that presenteeism – the phenomenon of being at work but not necessarily fully engaged – is estimated to cost Australian business alone almost $26 billion per year.

When I present leaders with the value of investing specifically in the growth and development of their team, I'm often told: 'But we have so much to do and so many stakeholders to please, such tight budgets, and pressure from the head office, that we don't have time for the *softer skills* stuff.'

My response is simple.

Building a Phenomenal Team has nothing to do with available time, and everything to do with what you *value*. Our choices regarding how we spend our time and where we spend our energy are based on what we value.

As leaders, we always have a choice as to where we spend our energy, and that choice will inevitably be driven by values.

Leaders who build Phenomenal Teams *value* the energy and time needed to invest in building their teams and the engagement of team members, because they know it ensures the sustainable success of the team. On the other hand, managers – dare I say it – value doing 'stuff', or being 'busy', or getting through a particular issue or through a difficult period of time.

Driving through tasks and ticking off the 'work-in-progress' list or getting through the 'to-do' list is the easy stuff!

Your team may have some of the core business practices and principles in place, or may be extremely talented, or may have agreement on their function. But unless you are making the ongoing, highly engaging review of what makes a Phenomenal Team a significant and regular part of your process and way of being, you may miss that pivotal moment in your team's life when an opportunity to be truly phenomenal comes along.

So, what does all this mean for *you*?

Firstly, all the evidence suggests that, more and more, people need to feel a sense of belonging within their community, and may well be getting frustrated by not finding this at the place where they spend much of their waking life: at work.

Secondly, it is my belief, built on years of observation and experience, that businesses and organisations can realise significant, sustainable growth with very little extra financial investment by simply focusing on the development and building of Phenomenal Teams. Doing this will lift the engagement and performance of team members.

People love being in teams. What a wonderful gift this is for the aspiring Legendary Leader!

People often define themselves by the team they are in, or the team they support, or the team they follow.

Imagine, just for a moment, that your legacy is the creation of an environment in which people feel safe, inspired, and empowered, and are obsessed with delivering phenomenal, sustained, benchmark performance.

What did I learn during my time as a senior manager and senior executive? In my desperate efforts to simply 'deliver the numbers', I missed the opportunity to create a truly Phenomenal Team. I know I certainly lost sleep during my time as a senior manager because of a number of issues, all of which related to the performance and sustainability of teams in my care.

Make no mistake, the process that moves teams toward being phenomenal will be challenging, but so is learning to ride a bike, or learning to surf, or learning to play a musical instrument – and I am sure you can appreciate how freeing, and exciting, and joyful it must feel once those skills are acquired!

This adventure is for the brave, the mavericks, the true believers, the ego-free, and the outliers. It will be ground-breaking, fear-facing, game-shaking, culture-making, truly awakening, pace-setting, true-believing and legacy-leaving ...

And it will be *so* rewarding!

This book will cover the key phases, stages, and questions you will need to ask yourself and your team, and the issues you may need to work through with your team. The process will provide insights into what has worked and what hasn't, and what you have to be careful of. And it will present a framework for building that Phenomenal Team and, in turn, helping *you* become that Legendary Leader.

By being brave and by continually aspiring to be that Legendary Leader who builds Phenomenal Teams that deliver sustainable, phenomenal success, your team will:

- feel safe to have the conversations that address the 'elephant in the room';
- agree to a team purpose that will ensure you are always growing;
- agree on which sustainable behaviours will drive successful delivery of your promise;
- activate these agreed behaviours and link them to performance and success;
- accelerate the growth of these behaviours;
- consistently and sustainably maximise engagement and performance; and
- deliver world's-best results – even without your continued involvement.

Through the process outlined in this book, you will also become aware of how you could develop as a leader. Remember – Phenomenal Teams are led by Legendary Leaders, and legends leave behind lots of leaders!

> *Phenomenal teams give us a purpose, a reason to stay connected, an opportunity to enrich each other and to meaningfully engage and, finally, a chance to amplify and magnify performance.*

Individual talent is an overvalued commodity. It is not only overvalued; it unfortunately doesn't last. Instead, harnessing the collective talent of your team will be the truly sustainable driver of performance.

It is my intent that, through the ideas presented in his book, creating Phenomenal Teams will become your leadership obsession.

People want to be in Phenomenal Teams. *Talent* wants to be in Phenomenal Teams. Talent *outside of your team* will want to be in your team. This is because talented people want to be stretched: they want to grow, they want to achieve amazing things, they want to be engaged and feel empowered.

It is this type of environment that could well be your legacy!

Are you ready?

HOW TO USE THIS BOOK

This book reflects how we would implement a Stretch to Grow High Performance Team Program in your organisation. The chapters pretty much follow the order in which we would build the platform for your team's growth toward becoming a phenomenal team.

However, this book is not a 'now do this' guide or a 'how-to' manual. Rather, think of this book as an opportunity to reflect on where your team is at right now and identify the area or areas that are either slowing down your team or provide a genuine growth opportunity.

My suggestion for working through the content is to identify the one (or two) key questions at the end of each chapter that you would really like the answer to, and to seek out other team members' thoughts on those questions.

I want you to stop and really reflect on the questions, especially the ones that make you feel a little uncomfortable when you think of the potential responses you might get from the rest of your team. In all likelihood, it is these questions, and the ensuing responses, that could very well have the biggest impact in shifting your team's openness to this adventure!

Who knows how much more your team is truly capable of if they were to aspire to be that phenomenal team.

I suggest that, once you've finished reading this book, you complete the Team Health Check found at the end of the book and ask your team members to independently complete it too. Include this in your team reflections and conversations, also. Specifically, replace your typical management meeting with an open discussion about where your team is at right now. I would also ask you to embrace the notion that building a phenomenal team is very doable – but you are going to need help!

Ultimately, it will come down to what you value as a leader, and how open you are to being guided through what will be a challenging, exciting, joyful, and rewarding adventure. I am sure you wouldn't try to climb Mount Everest without an experienced guide, so think of this book as the first step on that journey.

Please read, reflect, and engage others in your reflections. Be kind to yourself with the questions and answers, and then get really excited about how good your team could be!

Garie

PART ONE

WHY TEAMS MATTER

WHY TEAMS MATTER

often get a sense that people intuitively know what it takes to build high-performance teams. They might even feel they have been in one or were in one that almost hit the high-performance benchmark. But while many people feel that they have been in that high-performance team, they feel that they have been in some quite dysfunctional ones as well.

The problem we seem to have is isolating and articulating what is at the heart of that high-performing team. The challenge may well lie in how we bring all these collective experiences into one action-based framework.

Furthermore, if and when we are able to articulate it, how do we act on those fundamental differences between high-performing teams and dysfunctional ones? How can we use these learnings to start to act on where we believe or feel our team is at right now?

Outlining what is at the foundation of building your high-performance team is the focus of Part 1. Identifying and using some of the core elements that you will instinctively connect to, which characterise high-performance teams, may determine not only where your team is at right now, but what you may need to focus on to start your team's movement towards becoming not just *better*, but *the best.*

CHAPTER ONE

IT'S NOT ABOUT TALENT

et's open our adventure with a scenario that I have experienced from a few perspectives as a would-be leader, as a manager, as a participant, and as a facilitator.

I would like you to quietly nod your head if you have been part of this sort of experience.

You go away with your team for a couple of days, doing some cool and fun group-related activities (notice how I have deliberately avoided the word 'team-building'). This may have included some really challenging things like raft building, or rope climbing, or abseiling, or 'trust activities' involving falling backwards and hoping someone catches you, or even overnight camping with none of life's essentials.

You then go home at the end of the offsite, having had a great time and having high-fived and back-slapped all of the other team members, all ready and excited to get back to work the next week.

Unfortunately, though, after a couple of days back at work, you notice that you and possibly others are once again doing what you always did. You notice that you are still accepting and tolerating some non-productive behaviour, or not challenging or innovating as quickly as you would like, or you feel like the business has slowed. And by the way, you are still not getting on with that person in sales who always gets really agitated when commissions are due!

'So, what happened?' you ask yourself. 'We made a brilliant raft last week, and we climbed up all of those ropes, and then we abseiled down that cliff face ... I thought we had fixed all of our issues and had become a great team!'

No amount of overnighting, raft-building, rock-climbing, abseiling, storytelling, back-slapping, high-fiving investments will add any long-term value to your efforts to build a high-performance team.

The much-heralded two-day offsites will not ensure you are building a high-performance team. These activities are short term and while they may be motivational in the moment, conversations on key issues around performance may still be avoided once you return to your day-to-day environment.

The question is: 'Why?'

TRUST ME

To help us understand where the real issue may lie, let me relate a real exchange I once had with a client.

I was chatting with a senior manager in the construction industry about his team's performance. He was lamenting the fact that, despite his team having many years' experience and its members having great expertise, it consistently missed deadlines and delivery dates. Now, in the industry he was in, it was not unusual for missed deadlines or delivery dates to be accompanied by significant penalties.

After listening to his challenges, my response, much to his dismay, was to suggest that there may well be a trust issue in his team.

As you can imagine, the manager immediately defended the team by declaring, 'It can't be that simple, Garie. These are all good people.' I had to agree – they *were* good people! They were all trustworthy and, no doubt, had honest intentions when it came to work.

However, the trust issue I was alluding to was not related to the character of any individual team member, but rather to safety – the safety to challenge what was currently considered acceptable within this team.

I asked him, 'Do you think a couple of the people in the team actually know why they consistently miss deadlines?' The manager, rather reluctantly, acknowledged that there were people who may well know what the issues were.

So, why weren't they highlighting them? Why weren't they challenging the current work practices? And, most important of all, why weren't they implementing solutions and holding others to account?

What was stopping these people from saying anything, from giving their input and ideas, from challenging current practices or behaviours that should not have been tolerated? Simply put: It was not safe to speak up.

Those people did not trust that their observations or comments could be heard without penalty – particularly by senior team members. They were worried about the ramifications to them if they *did* speak up. There was a culture in this team that did not reward those who challenged the established ways of working – even if those ways of working were inefficient, unsafe, or unprofitable.

In fact, it is highly likely that there was a culture that supported, and therefore rewarded, team members who *avoided* challenging the accepted ways of doing things.

With this story in mind, let's go back to the week after that wonderful offsite, when you observed that nothing had really changed. It may well be that your organisation's environment or culture is not based on safety, accountability, and performance. It may not be safe to challenge behaviours, work practices, or ways of doing things. And unfortunately, a couple of days away will not fix these trust issues.

The building of trust is at the very heart of building high-performance environments and teams.

Trust is the foundation stone of any attempts we make at building a phenomenal team. The building of trust will accelerate your movement toward having that phenomenal team, which is led by many, and which will, in turn, accelerate and amplify your team's performance.

THE IMPACT OF TRUST

Much has been written, and equal amounts of evidence gathered, showing the relationship between trust and speed – in other words, that performance is quicker when there are high levels of trust. We can link economic reality to the existence (or not) of trust.

Hence, the cost or impact of not building high levels of trust in your team will show up in many ways.

People's time is expensive. The time you allocate to dealing with issues that others won't deal with is expensive. Having to continually redo projects, or to start them only to have to change course because they weren't planned well enough or the barriers and solutions were insufficiently discussed, is expensive. And in the case of the real example we opened the chapter with, missing deadlines or not delivering on time is expensive.

Poor or inconsistent teams are characterised by really low levels of trust. Phenomenal teams move quicker because it is safe to address issues quickly.

Let's look at Figure 1 to help us understand.

Figure 1: The Trust Pyramid

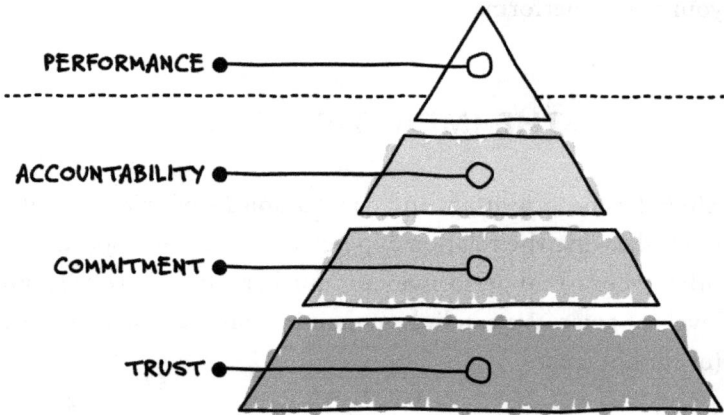

The pyramid has long been viewed as one of the most enduring man-made structures because of the strength of its foundations.

Trust is at the foundation of your team's growth. The building of trust will ensure that your team has a solid and sustainable foundation for growth.

By building high levels of *trust*, team members *commit* both to the team and, of equal importance, to each other. They don't want to let each other or the team down. They take the team's performance personally.

As a consequence, they welcome being held *accountable*, and are equally comfortable holding others to account. It is safe to address issues affecting the team's performance.

They trust the intent of their teammates, and they trust that any feedback or conversations they have with their teammates will be taken in the right spirit and with an understanding that this is about the team's performance.

The result is inevitable improvement in performance.

Trust will be the foundation on which your team's performance and growth will be built.

UNDERSTANDING THE CASH MACHINE

I am sure you know people who have gone to withdraw money from an ATM and been confronted with the unsettling words 'Insufficient funds'.

The building of trust is no different.

To ensure there is trust, you need to make deposits of trust every day, for there may – in fact, there most likely will – come a day when you need to withdraw some of those funds.

Trust is not built in a day, but it is built daily!

We all mess up at some time, and when we do, we inevitably have to withdraw some of that trust from our account. What we need to ensure is that we have plenty of trust deposited in the bank when we make that withdrawal.

Equally, you may have to challenge a long-established operating process, or a senior person's behaviour. If the trust levels are high – that is, lots of deposits in the trust ATM – this conversation will be welcomed. If not?

Well, at this point, it is not unusual for me to be told: 'We *do* have high levels of trust in this team; we all get on really well!'

Trust, and therefore safety, is less about getting on with each other at a superficial level than it is about feeling safe enough to address those key issues and challenges that exist in the operating methods and behaviours that may well be stopping you and your team from growing.

One of the challenges you may have when looking to build higher levels of trust in your team is embracing the notion that building meaningful working relationships adds far more value than 'getting on well'.

The building of meaningful working relationships is really the key step in building high levels of trust.

If trust is the foundation of your team's performance, then the building of meaningful working relationships is the mortar that holds that foundation together.

BUILDING RELATIONSHIPS

Imagine that tomorrow you are going to be brave and actually stop to check in with that person you typically just acknowledge. What would be safe to talk about and wouldn't give too much away, but would be better than the 'grunt' you have been using for the past six months and would at least move the relationship along?

I am sure the inevitable topics come to mind – the weather, sport, television, celebrity gossip, and the age-old classic: 'How was your weekend?'! Certainly, all good starting points. But they are only starting points.

It is also not unusual for the question 'How is work?' to pop up at this level. Is that meaningful? No. You're just *acknowledging* that person.

I have seen a wink, a thumb in the air, a nod of the head, or, in some environments the all-purpose response: 'Mate!'

The next level of engagement, beyond just acknowledgement, tends to be characterised by *asking*, or, in some cases, *telling* someone about a work-related issue, while not genuinely caring about the response.

Is this building a meaningful working relationship? No!

I once heard someone in a workshop that I was facilitating suggest that they had a meaningful working relationship with a person in another department 'because they always do what I need them to do when I'm in a hurry'! This sounded a little self-serving and was very much in the 'telling' space.

I also had a senior manager claim that they could have the conversation around performance with anyone in the room. However, when I asked the rest of the team if they felt the same way toward this manager, not one person felt that *they* could have the same conversation with *him*.

Simply feeling safe to *tell* people something is not a conversation that builds trust.

Once you move beyond telling, you actually start to ask more questions, and start to truly *seek* answers.

At this level, you are seeking to understand the reasons *why* the other person had a great weekend or *why* they are so busy or tired, and you may even seek out and share ways you could help them with their workload. You are seeking to *understand* what is going on behind their initial response.

It is in this phase that trust starts to be built, and we start to *share*.

Both you and your fellow team member now feel safe bringing up the real issues and sharing your thoughts – sharing how you're really feeling, sharing the fact that you need help, sharing your confusion with where the business is going. You may even be able to share how the other's behaviour is having an impact on *your* performance and the performance of the team. When trust is built, these become common conversations.

> *Seeking to understand why someone chooses a particular behaviour and sharing with them the impact it is having on you and others is a far richer and more valuable conversation, in terms of building trust, than just telling them they need to change.*

A simple starting point in the building of meaningful working relationships is to have the conversations around, rather than giving a directive about, your expectations of each other.

STOP AND REFLECT

In meaningful working relationships, both parties *really* feel:

- valued and respected;
- understood, appreciated, and aware of a shared set of values and experiences; and
- safe to be vulnerable and to share and seek.

And they can *really*:

- talk openly about how they feel;

- define and share their own values, beliefs and principles, and align their behaviour to them; and
- articulate what is acceptable in the relationship and what they expect from each other in the relationship.

So, stop and think about the key relationships that you need to have in your team right now, and maybe reflect on these two sets of key elements.

Could each member of your team genuinely say 'yes' to each of these key elements when discussing their relationship with other members of the team? Could you?

Phenomenal teams have these wonderful, rich conversations regularly to ensure that trust levels are continually growing.

If conversations are being avoided, then there is every chance one (or more) of these key elements is missing, or not being genuinely felt to the extent you may be assuming it is.

On a day-to-day, moment-to-moment basis, your investment in the building of meaningful working relationships will only serve to strengthen the levels of trust in your team's environment.

Having conversations that increase your understanding of where team members are at is vital to getting to the heart of this.

Some members of the team may need clarity of the *vision*, or their role in the delivery of the *purpose*, or even their *key performance indicators* (KPIs). They may need to get agreement from you about what you expect from them and which behaviours are aligned with the team's values, and, equally important, team members may need the opportunity to outline what *they* expect from *you* as their leader.

You may need to understand team members' learning styles – some team members may need clearly defined processes and systems, and some may need a forum to express all of their wonderful ideas for new ways of working they have been dreaming about!

Addressing, recognising, and implementing all these elements serve to strengthen the relationships and, subsequently, that foundation of trust.

Building meaningful working relationships builds a feeling of safety and value, and it is this feeling of safety that truly reflects and impacts the level of trust in your team.

TIME OUT TO TALK ABOUT:

- Where do you really think the level of trust is in your team right now?

- How safe do you think it is in your team right now?

- Do all members of your team challenge the status quo and offer new solutions?

- Do you have the conversations that really matter around individual and team performance?

- Do you feel as though your team has slowed down?

- Where are your relationships with each team member relative to the circle of trust?

- Do you ask to speak, or ask to seek?

- Do you know what drives, motivates, or scares each member of your team?

- Do you ignore small issues because you are 'too busy' or 'doing well'?

CHAPTER TWO

HOW SUCCESSFUL COULD WE BE?

When meeting leaders for the first time, one of the key elements I listen for is the language they use to describe their team's performance. I am specifically listening for how that leader describes the team's 'currency'.

I define 'currency' as the language or words the leader, and consequently the team members, use to validate themselves, justify themselves, trade on, or use as capital.

My conversation with a leader may well start with:

- 'I couldn't ask any more from my team at the moment – we are all working so hard'; or
- 'We have so much talent but ... '; or
- 'We are a great team. Last year was our best year ever. It's just that this year we have had a few challenges working against us, and now ... '

And then there's:

- 'We are a great team. We get on so well. And so, I don't understand why we aren't growing or improving'; or
- 'It is a little too early to tell. We have only just been pulled together.'

Let's reflect on some of these comments.

- 'Too early to tell' suggests that 'getting to know each other' is the currency.
- 'We get on well' suggests that harmony is the currency.
- 'We are all working really hard' suggests that 'effort or output' is the currency.

If you reflect on what you or your team members talk about a lot, what would you say is your team's currency?

WHAT IS YOUR VALUE?

From my experience, clearly understanding and accepting where your team is at right now, and what the shift in currency needs to be, is the most revealing and impactful start to your adventure.

To help clarify where you are at, have a look at Table 1: Team Value Ladder. This highlights the hierarchy of team performance, the value such teams bring to the organisation, and the potential for ongoing success.

Table 1: Team Value Ladder

PHENOMENAL TEAMS	
Leaders	Many, and many more on the way
Trust levels	Extremely high
Performance	Consistently exceed expectations
Currency	• Being world's best / benchmark. • Purpose as the driver of strategy and all actions
Ongoing success rate	90% to 100%
GREAT TEAMS	
Leaders	Quite a few
Trust levels	Very high
Performance	Consistently hits the mark, now and then exceeds
Currency	• Delivering on its purpose • Continual improvement
Ongoing success rate	70% to 80%
GOOD TEAMS	
Leaders	One obvious leader and one or two with potential
Trust levels	Inconsistent
Performance	Hits the mark now and then ('moment in the sun')
Currency	• Working hard to get things done
Ongoing success rate	40% to 50%
FAKE TEAMS	
Leaders	One hierarchical leader, like captain or manager
Trust levels	Really low
Performance	Consistently misses, but it's 'never their fault'
Currency	• Harmony
Ongoing success rate	20% (at best!)
FALSE TEAMS	
Leaders	Not yet
Trust levels	Low, but with good intent
Performance	Too early to tell
Currency	• Getting to know each other
Ongoing success rate	0% to 10%

Have a look at the Team Value Ladder and give some thought to where your team REALLY is, not where you think (or hope) it is.

What do you see, hear, know, or feel right now about your team?

Upon looking at the Team Value Ladder, your natural reaction may well be to suggest that you and your team are in the *good* or even *great* tiers – or even a mixture of *good* and *great*. I have had occasions where team members will review the characteristics of a good team and those of a great team, and immediately conclude that they are a great team because they can tick off three of the key elements. Unfortunately, you need all of them!

That is not to say, though, that if you already have some of the aspirational traits, you shouldn't articulate these, and recognise them, and use them as building blocks to accelerate your upward movement.

If you have had some really strong years but have now slipped, then you are a *good* team that was approaching *great*, not a *great* team that has slipped.

Let's have a look at the stages in a little more detail, with a particular focus on what you would see or hear if you were in a team that was at that stage.

1. FALSE TEAMS

At this stage, the team leader could well be the person that pulled this group of highly skilled people together. It may be the leader has been appointed as CEO or general manager in a new business. This leader may be leading a specific project team, or a new sales team, or a collective of people with a specific, short-term goal.

Typically, at this stage, there is no real clarity on the purpose of the team (other than a functional one) or its agreed behaviours. Trust levels will be relatively low, but with good intentions.

Often, when asked how the team is going, the response may be, 'A little too early to tell. We are only just getting to know each other and to understand our roles' or 'We are still working through what success looks like for us'. The challenge here is to ensure you don't stay in this phase for too long!

In elite sport in particular, we know when a team – or more specifically its leader – is stuck in this space and may in fact be using it as an excuse for non-performance.

'We are in a re-building phase' or 'This is a period of transition for us' are typical clichés rolled out when the leader has failed to get the team through this phase.

QUESTIONS TO ASK

- What language do I hear used when we describe ourselves?
- Is it clear what our purpose is, what our plan is, and what success looks like for us?

---

2. FAKE TEAMS

This stage is clearly identified by the language used when discussing progress on a project, or sales targets, or delivery timeframes, or performance.

Fake teams use *harmony* as their currency.

Inevitably in the fake team, due to low levels of trust, issues and conflict are avoided, and 'blame, complain and defend' behaviours and language are tolerated. No one is willing to take responsibility for not performing or delivering.

I assume that you can now appreciate why I specifically asked you to continually work to build trust within your team. It is only by building a safe, trusting environment that you can have these *real* conversations about where your team is at. And it is by reaching agreement across the team about where your starting point is that you will ensure you have every opportunity to become that phenomenal team.

Unfortunately, the recurring conversations go a little like this:

- 'If we could only get marketing to deliver this for us';

- 'We need senior management to give us a voice';
- 'The customer keeps delaying a decision and wants more';
- 'We can't compete with our competitor's pricing ... it's Customer Services' fault,' (if you are the Sales Team);
- It's the Sales Team's fault,' (if you are the Customer Service team);
- 'The external market has changed now and we need *this* to happen ... ';

... and so on. Do you get the idea?

Fake teams live in a blame, complain, and defend cycle. Quite unconsciously, in most cases, teams like this start to present themselves as victims. And guess who allows that? Yes, the hierarchical leader!

In fact, the term *hierarchical leader* may be an oxymoron. Fake teams do not have a leader in the true sense of the word. They tend to have a hierarchical *head*, for example a 'Head of *x*'.

If we accept the notion that teams look like their leaders, then there is a very strong chance that the senior person designated to lead this team is tolerating, accepting, and quite conceivably fuelling and buying into this blame-complain-defend culture.

And herein lies a really disturbing element within fake teams. Because the appointed (or hierarchical) lead may not be conscious of this blame-complain-defend culture, or has chosen to ignore it, or worse still, may in fact be actively engaged in it, leadership within this team actually starts to resemble the blame-complain-defend dialogue.

What is accepted in this team when we discuss our performance? Blame, complain, defend: it is never 'our fault'!

The disturbing outcome? No real, action-based, forward-thinking, accountable leaders emerge.

As long as everyone gets on and there is someone or something external to blame, then this type of team will always find a reason for not achieving its objectives. And if this culture is accepted, then it may well define leadership.

Even though individual team members may be extremely skilled in their role, it's at this point, when conversations are avoided and genuine trust levels are low (although likability is important), that any remedial action is slow to initiate. Or indeed it may never take place.

Consequently, this team moves slowly and is allowed, and at times encouraged, to get distracted.

*The **fake team** is very happy to talk about others, even while knowing that they really do need to talk about themselves first and foremost, but do not feel safe or supported in doing so.*

QUESTIONS TO ASK

- Do we get caught up in issues that we cannot control?
- Is there always an external reason for us not performing?
- Are there any 'elephants in the room'?

---

3. GOOD TEAMS

One of the stand-out attributes of *good* teams is that, every now and then, they have this wonderful moment in the sun!

Unfortunately, that moment is not sustainable, and will then be followed by periods of non-performance, despite the fact that team members will often harken back to that moment of glory.

I once worked with a rugby league team who had some influential players convinced that they were a great team. Consequently, they were resistant to the notion that they had a fair bit of work to do.

Once they accepted that they had only won the Premiership once in forty-odd years and hadn't played in a Grand Final since, they were alerted to the slightly delusional point they had gotten to.

They were a good team that had managed to maximise a single moment.

In the *good* team, the leader tends to be hierarchical and is the one often left to have the conversations about performance. The team may have a set of agreed values, but they are rarely – if ever – used to drive performance. In some instances, these values may only be seen when it comes time for performance reviews.

Equally, it is not unusual in the corporate environment for this team to be made up of various 'Heads of'. Desired behaviours, and even team purpose, are occasionally referenced, but are often neglected in favour of functional delivery. For example, 'I know the behaviour isn't quite what we are looking for, but wow – can they sell!'

As with the *fake* team, one of the consequences of being in a *good* team is that leadership behaviour becomes a little blurred. The conversations around performance may be left to senior members of the team, and trust levels are mixed.

In short, there is not a demonstrated understanding that delivering on the agreed behaviours is how they will deliver on the agreed business outcomes.

> *In **good** teams, delivery of the business outcomes is the currency, and will therefore take precedence over the purpose and behaviours.*

QUESTIONS TO ASK

- When we meet, is the singular focus on *doing* and delivering one (or maybe two) key business outcomes?
- Are meetings simply a summary of all the work we have in progress?
- Do we ever use our purpose as the starting point for solutions?

4. GREAT TEAMS

As opposed to being consumed with just being super busy 'doing', teams in the *great* space get that it is about 'who they need to *be*' rather than what they need to *do*.

Asking this question is also no longer the exclusive domain of the designated leader. Quite a few in the team will be driving this real conversation.

Clearly, leadership now looks like 'living the agreed behaviours'.

A very clear, articulated connection is made between performance and behaviour, and every outcome, tactic, and strategy needs to link and reinforce the agreed purpose (or promise) of the team or organisation.

Behaviour is always reviewed as part of the team performance schedule, with real and timely conversations about rewarding those behaviours that are aligned with the team's agreement.

Equally, non-productive behaviour is addressed quickly and directly.

Trust levels are now high, with meaningful working relationships taking priority over friendships. As a consequence, issues get sorted quickly and real conversations are quickly had by many in the team, with actions as the outcome.

We now see a demonstrated balance and an understanding that delivering on the behaviours actually assures delivery of the fundamentals.

The currency now moves beyond just delivery and on to behaviour-based questions like:

- What would we need to do or add to be even better at delivering on our purpose than we were last month?
- What would it take for you to do or be better than last month?
- What would we need to do or add for us to be the best our industry?
- What I have noticed, though, with great teams, is that they tend to only last as long as the core team members remain.

How often have you heard 'Oh, that great marketing team? That was in the Mary Smith and John Jones era!'

Great teams tend to be 'era based'.
How long have you got left?

QUESTIONS TO ASK

- Do we have our purpose as the starting point for all our conversations or meetings?
- Would the performance of this team slip if I lost my two or three best leaders?
- Do we consistently exceed performance expectations and do we have a balanced focus on growth, both of our people and the business?

5. PHENOMENAL TEAMS

Simply put, *phenomenal* teams are led by many. The next leader, and wave of leaders, are continually being identified, developed, and added.

At any point in time *any* member of the team will feel safe enough to own, lead, drive, challenge, recognise, and reward. Any member is comfortable with proactively identifying opportunities, highlighting issues and challenges, or initiating projects.

Phenomenal delivery on the purpose and exceptional delivery of the behaviours by all now becomes the priority and is the single biggest driver of growth and performance.

This team becomes obsessed with looking at how they can amplify their purpose or promise, to the point where they continually amaze others by what they achieve. Targets become nearly irrelevant!

The constant, driving question in a phenomenal team is: 'Who do we need to be right now, and how can we amplify this?'

What is also noticeable here is that these are the teams that everyone wants to be on! And those already on one will do everything they can to stay on it.

Performance, and the accompanying currency, are now measured against the world's best, regardless of the market segment or even industry. In fact, it is these teams that transcend their industry.

QUESTIONS TO ASK

- Could any person in our team step into the structural leader's role today without reducing our success?
- Is our team exceeding expectations and, if so, is that sustainable?
- Are all team members developing and growing their successors?

THE JOURNEY TO PHENOMENAL

I have lost count of the number of corporate leaders who have read a book about the success of the New Zealand All Blacks and then want their teams to be just like them. They're especially keen on the observation that the senior All Blacks players clean the dressing rooms!

It is only after I highlight the fact that the All Blacks are obsessed with identifying and developing future leaders, and that their success is not just a matter of cleaning their own dressing rooms, that these leaders realise the true depth of the challenge.

In fact, I highlight the fact that I once worked with a rugby league team that cleaned their own dressing rooms, and they finished thirteenth on the ladder!

Members of phenomenal teams feel like leaders: highly valued, purposeful, and certain. They are consistently successful, by any measure you wish to use. They feel safe having any type of conversations and are obsessed with and focused on improving performance.

Understanding, listening for, and highlighting your team's currency is key to understanding where you may need to start in transforming your team into a phenomenal one.

It is only by constantly and consistently checking in on the key elements in the Value Ladder that you will be able to genuinely address performance and measure sustainable improvements.

*Then, and only then, can you learn how to ensure you don't just **achieve** phenomenal status, but **stay** there ... which is exactly what we'll do next.*

TIME OUT TO TALK ABOUT:

- What currency do you think your team uses?

- How many genuine leaders do you have in your team?

- Do you find yourself spending far too much time on 'micro' issues?

- At which stage of the Value Ladder is your team?

- What critical elements are missing in your team?

- How confident are you of the ongoing success of your team should you move on?

PART TWO

THE KEYS TO PHENOMENAL TEAMS

THE KEYS TO PHENOMENAL TEAMS

N ow that you know *why* your team needs to become, and stay, phenomenal, how can you go about making that happen?

There is a general rule for team growth that looks like this:

$$P = C^3$$

P IS THE TEAM'S PURPOSE (OR PROMISE TO THE ORGANISATION).

In simple terms, do you and your team have clarity and agreement on 'Why we are here?' The answer to this question will become the guiding light for the team and the conversation goes beyond, 'What is our function?'

Phenomenal teams are purpose driven. All their strategies, plans, behaviours and conversations serve to drive, amplify and accelerate their *purpose*.

The delivery of the purpose will be the multiplier of three things – the three Cs of the team growth equation: commitment, credibility, and conversations.

1. COMMITMENT

What is the set of behaviours that your team will agree on and commit to that will ensure you deliver on your purpose?

The behaviours you reward, recognise, and tolerate are evidence of the culture of your team. If you accept this, then you need to commit to a team culture that will ensure you are able to deliver on your promise.

This part of the process really does highlight the notion that you cannot *be* the same team you have been in the past if you want to be phenomenal.

2. CREDIBILITY

The key question here relates very much to the delivery and performance aspect of your team and is triggered by asking: 'What plans and/or processes do we need to have in place to ensure this team has credibility?' Put another way, 'What are the fundamental business elements that need to be in place for you to maximise the impact on your purpose?'

3. CONVERSATIONS

Great and *phenomenal* teams meet regularly to have conversations that may include debate – sometimes conflict, and sometimes agreement – on the *real* issues. These are the real conversations. What you *need* to talk about takes priority over what you are *happy* to talk about.

When phenomenal teams are driven by this rule and bring all of these elements together, they become FAAST. They are flexible, accountable, aspirational, strategic, and tight, as shown in Figure 2.

Figure 2: Becoming FAAST

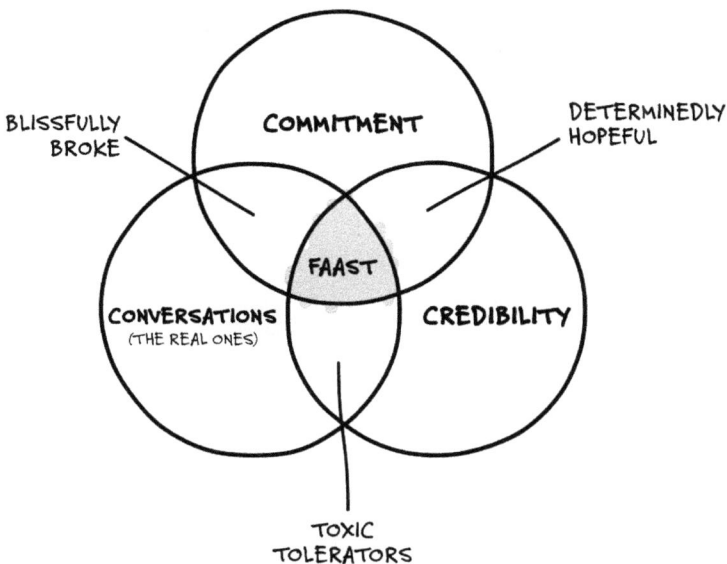

BLISSFULLY BROKE

COMMITMENT

DETERMINEDLY HOPEFUL

FAAST

CONVERSATIONS (THE REAL ONES)

CREDIBILITY

TOXIC TOLERATORS

Let's look at how to become FAAST, starting with identifying your purpose.

CHAPTER THREE

GET PURPOSEFUL WITH YOUR PROMISE

I used to have difficulty with the notion that cricket was a team sport.

I used to view it more as a collective of individuals with highly specialised skills who were required to deliver on their specialty, and the winner of a particular encounter was the team that had the best collective total of the specialties. (I have come across some teams in the corporate environment that actually *do* look a little like this.)

My thoughts were that unless you were a really good batter or bowler, there wasn't much else you could do to contribute to the success of the team. I wasn't seeing anyone getting picked because they were a great fielder.

Now, let me share a story that not only exposes my ignorance, but unequivocally proves that this view is naïve.

I have been working with an elite cricket team recently, and my engagement coincided with the appointment of a new head coach who came after a review of the team's progress and performance.

The principal challenge was that despite having an impressively deep talent pool, this team had not played in a Sheffield Shield final – the ultimate prize for state cricket teams – for five seasons. This was an almost unprecedented situation, given their talent and prior history.

What became clear was that *talent* wasn't the issue. What the head coach had picked up on and I, in turn, supported, was that the players had never really given much thought to, or been challenged on, why they were actually there.

What was the team's fundamental reason for being?

The obvious response from a few when asked this question was 'to win cricket games' or 'to win the Sheffield Shield'. That clearly, however, wasn't really connecting with the players. Their performance had been below expectations and at times the team dynamic was dysfunctional, particularly when it became evident that they were not going to win the Sheffield Shield.

So, our starting point was to stretch the players' thinking in relation to their *Why*? Why was winning games of cricket or the Sheffield Shield important?

The coach and a handful of senior players were pivotal to this process. The coach proceeded to take the players away for two days with the primary purpose of establishing the team's *Why*.

And establish it they did.

The *team purpose*, which has become the team's guiding star, is now the platform for agreeing on and establishing the behaviours that are rewarded, and the context for broader conversations around performance.

Skill and delivery of each member's respective speciality is important, but equally important is the way each player goes about their day-to-day engagement and contribution to the team purpose.

Winning games, winning teams, or winning the Sheffield Shield merely serve as indicators that the team is building toward a bigger future.

In the two seasons since undertaking this exercise, with senior players developing as leaders and driving this process with the support of the head coach and his coaching team, this team has now not only *played* in a Sheffield Shield final, they've *won* a Sheffield Shield.

Hence, everything your players do, and every challenge they face – whether on or off the field, in the boardroom, at practice, or in the weights room – is connected to delivering on your team's overall purpose.

FROM THE FIELD TO THE BOARDROOM

With the story of the cricket team in mind, let's translate the concepts into a corporate environment.

Imagine there are two teams in your organisation, Team One and Team Two as described below in Table 2.

Table 2: Two Types of Teams

TEAM ONE	TEAM TWO
• A group of well-intentioned team members who have a good understanding of the details of their own roles and business units. • Spends very little time, if any, on why the team exists or what values or behaviours should drive success or have been missed when projects aren't successful. • Talks about being strategic, but members can't really articulate a simple, clear strategy. • Consistently managing against a long list of eclectic goals, some of which may not be compatible and may only pertain to individual team members. • Team members have limited knowledge about (or interest in) the responsibilities or challenges of their peers.	• Team members share a common passion and are committed to abiding by the same set of values and behaviours. • Has a clear plan for success and knows exactly how it differs from that of the competition. • At any given moment, can articulate its overarching purpose, supporting strategy, and top collective priorities. Members understand how each contributes to achieving those priorities. • Priorities are clearly linked to a longer-term, collective vision.

What do you notice about the two teams?
*Where do you think **your** team currently sits?*

When presented with these two options, it is not unusual for leaders and team members to take the middle ground and suggest that they are a mix of the two.

Equally, some teams will go straight to Team One and acknowledge it with comments like 'How did you know?' or 'Have you been at some of our meetings?'

Team One is not necessarily in a bad place. They may be quite a good team and may eventually deliver on their objectives, goals, or projects. But for how long, and at what cost? Is the performance thanks to one or two individuals, and is the performance sustainable?

There are also teams who will say that they have a common commitment and are passionate about the same thing, until I ask them to write down independently what that is, and we compare each team member's thoughts.

*The key element missing in Team One is **clarity of purpose** – why does the team exist, and what is it really that its members are all truly committed to?*

What sets Team Two apart is the link between why they are there and their action plans.

Team Two can link their action plans and strategy directly to the team's reason for being – its purpose.

The team's purpose reflects the team members' idealistic moti-vations for doing the work. It doesn't just describe outputs; it captures the soul of the team.

It is only when the team thinks beyond their function, and has agreement and clarity on why it is here, that team members will care about each other, care about the team, be able to clearly articulate and connect the strategy or priorities, and be genuinely strategic.

Without connecting all strategic thinking to *the why*, any idea will be a great one, or any behaviour will be acceptable, as long as it helps us get what we need to get!

Simon Sinek observed that 'Very few companies can clearly articulate *why* they do *what* they do.'

From my experience, what appears to be at the heart of a team's failure to stay focused and to continually bring all strategic thinking back to *the why* is the lack of a common purpose or sense of belonging that transcends function, and speaks to the personal and emotional connection of the team members.

Your team's purpose articulates the unique gift it brings to the organisation.

Purpose also serves as the launching pad for action and is the mirror that the team should look in when it's not delivering on its performance indicators.

Of equally importance, it is what the team emotionally connects to. It is its reason for being, and in phenomenal teams is often at the core of why team members are prepared to give the discretionary effort that sets the team apart.

BECOMING PURPOSE DRIVEN

Too often, when teams are faced with a challenge – whether it be missing sales targets, delays delivering on a project, or not meeting customer expectations – the immediate response is to go straight to building an action plan and, with admirable intent, the team gets busy trying to fix what it believes is holding it back.

'I don't have time to meet Garie. We are frantic and overwhelmed right now just trying to come up with ways to sort this problem out', or words to this effect, is the common response.

Without a purpose at the heart of what the team needs to be, it's not uncommon for team members to become somewhat frantic or confused or 'busy' when faced with challenges.

I have witnessed this first-hand, even when the team purpose is plastered all over the wall!

The phenomenal team will go straight to 'Which part of our purpose aren't we delivering or focused on and why?'

Assuming high levels of trust and safety, this question provides the opportunity to get to the truth, align resources, align behaviour, and ensure the team establishes clear priorities to move beyond the current issue.

On the other hand, teams who go straight to the doing, without reflecting on its purpose, may spend enormous amounts of effort on tasks that may or may not address the issue. Consequently, it may turn into a team that is in no way representative of its true potential.

Our priority, then, is to establish the purpose of your team, as this becomes what you hold yourself and your team accountable to.

To help you identify your purpose, ask yourself these questions:

1. **What are some of your leadership moments?**
   Think of moments in the past when you have been really proud to be a member (or leader) of your team. Jot down the details. For example: '*I was really proud to be a member of the leadership team when we overdelivered all our results last financial year.*'

   If you're having trouble identifying moments like this, imagine moments in the future that, from a leadership perspective, *would* make you really proud to be a member of this team.

2. **What actions did you take?**
   What did your team need to do (what actions needed

to be taken) for you to realise this or these moment(s)? For example: '*We had to create clarity on the strategy, get people to buy in, give people the opportunity to be innovative, and let some people run a little freer than usual.*'

3. **What impact did it have on others?**
   What did (or would) these actions enable people to feel or do? For example: '*It made people in the team (or in the business) feel engaged and empowered, and enabled them to really step up and own the project.*'

4. **What did the team 'get' as a result?**
   What were the tangible results of these actions for the team? For example: '*The team was given more responsibility and/or more resources to accomplish its goals in the next financial year.*'

We now have the raw ingredients to start moulding our purpose as a leadership team.

BRINGING IT ALL TOGETHER

I have noticed that the purpose has the most impact when it is broken down into three key aspects:

1. What is the action?
2. What feelings must be activated?
3. What is the desired outcome?

Using the example from above, we could start to see that the purpose of this leadership team could well be something along the lines of:

Our purpose, as a leadership team, is to create clarity (the action), so that our people have a sense of ownership and feel empowered and engaged (the feelings) to deliver beyond expectations (the outcome).

It is indeed aspirational, as, I believe, the team's purposes *should* be. It also needs to be a constant driver – you need a mindset that suggests this is never done. The purpose will guide and inspire team members and will be forever pursued.

The other key question that a strong purpose evokes is: 'Does this inspire change?'

If the team were to embrace this purpose, does it naturally follow that it will need to *be* a different team?

Through these steps, it is hoped that team members will start to actually feel and embrace the higher-level impact they can have in light of this purpose.

The purpose becomes what the leadership team promises to deliver for the organisation. It is the leadership team's gift back to the broader team or organisation.

ENGAGING YOUR PROMISE

We have touched on the word 'engagement' within this example of team purpose (your promise back to the organisation or group of people you are intending to inspire). This is quite deliberate, as engagement is probably the key outcome of getting your purpose clear and, more important, it is a very real part of how you operate.

From my experience, engagement is the principal reason team members consistently give the discretionary effort that, more often than not, gives the phenomenal team the edge, as shown in Figure 3. It is the effort that team members give when they don't really have to. In fact, in the phenomenal environment, there are times when this discretionary effort is given, yet the team member is not even aware of it!

Figure 3: Engaging the Purpose

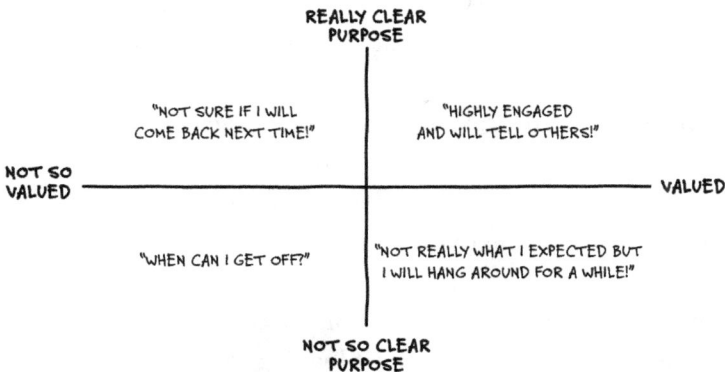

Looking at Figure 3, it is clear that engagement is maximised when team members are absolutely clear on *why* they are there and how the execution of their role will affect the purpose, and when they feel really valued in the delivery of their role.

> *Engagement is at risk, no matter how highly valued the team member feels, if clarity of purpose is missing.*

Engagement is like a boat cruise that you're invited to join.

The invitation promises an exciting destination and luxury treatment for the duration of the cruise.

Now, imagine the cruise provides everything that was promised. You are treated really well, with constant communication from the crew who check in to see that you have everything you need. Imagine what happens to your engagement levels. They may be so high that you tell lots of other people about the wonderful cruise when you return, and you are more than likely to come back next year should you be invited again!

What happens, though, if you are treated well but the location isn't really what was promised? You may grin and bear it, but you may also warn others to be careful and you might not be keen to go again next year.

And what if neither the care nor the destination was up to scratch? This is when you start looking to get off the boat as soon as possible!

Finally, how do you feel if the destination was exactly as you were promised, but you didn't feel particularly special during the trip. Would you return? You may give it one more go, but I am sure you will have mixed feelings.

Without purpose, your cruise doesn't really have a destination, so it is hard for your guests to feel their contribution it is valued!

However, with agreement and clarity of purpose, and therefore clarity on what you promise as a team to focus on, your ship returns to port full of high-spirited, excited (and possibly exhausted) guests. They cannot wait to go on the cruise again and will be raving fans of the experience!

TIME OUT TO TALK ABOUT:

- When your team faces challenges, do you and your team talk about 'what we have to do', or 'who we have to be?'

- If you do have a purpose? How aspirational is it?

- What do you use as your 'springboard to action'?

- Could each member of your team clearly articulate the same purpose when asked 'What is the purpose of this team?'

- Does your strategy serve to amplify your purpose?

- What is your team's promise back to the organisation?

- Are your current performance indicators linked to your purpose?

- How truly engaged are your team members?

CHAPTER FOUR

MAKE A COMMITMENT

et me share an example of a common problem that leaders face once the team has established its higher-level purpose.

This particular leader realised that in order for the organisation to grow, address challenges from the competition and the current operating environment, and shift strategic direction, a significant cultural change was needed.

The leader also acknowledged that, when talking about 'cultural change', what is meant is 'a shift in behaviours'. The organisation was going to have to move away from behaviours that had previously been rewarded, tolerated, and recognised.

The starting point was to establish a purpose for the whole team. It had become apparent that team members were unclear as to why they were there. More importantly, the reasons they believed they were there focused on the individual, not the team.

My role was to pull this purpose together over a two-day workshop involving nearly all members of the Australian sales and operations team.

At the end of the two days, the team had agreed on its purpose, had committed to a promise back to the organisation, had identified the key indicators that would test the delivery of the purpose, and had experienced a number of 'light bulb' moments.

Fast forward six weeks, when the group was brought back together to test, review, and strengthen the delivery of that purpose ...

The team's biggest concern at the start of this review? Nothing had changed in terms of the counterproductive behaviour prevalent in the business! In fact, some of the more mischievous team members were using the purpose as justification for their behaviour.

I then asked the group to think about a number of key questions, and to predict how others might answer them. Then I asked them to reflect on and capture how they were being seen by others, and what others would see as the key behaviours that were being rewarded and recognised.

The result was, as you can imagine, illuminating to say the least. There were a number of takeaways that the team reflected and built on, but in the context of the next stage of the team's development, there was one key takeaway that clearly had to become a priority.

The team realised, through this series of conversations, that their behaviours were in no way aligned with their agreed purpose, despite feeling within *themselves* that they were living their purpose.

> *There was a realisation within the team that its commitment to its purpose was ultimately reflected by how its members behaved, what they tolerated, both from each other and from others in the business, and what they valued.*

What was clearly missing for the team was clarity on which behaviours were most aligned with the delivery of the purpose, and therefore which should be the key behaviours that were rewarded and recognised.

This combination of purpose and aligned behaviours constitutes the *team brand*, and ultimately the strength of your team brand lies in what others say about you, not what you say about yourselves or have written on the wall.

So, once individuals had established who they had to be, and which behaviours reflected this, they could be rewarded, recognised, and challenged relative to their commitment to displaying these behaviours.

The strength of your team's brand ultimately lies in consistent delivery on a core set of behaviours that you have agreed are imperative in the delivery of your purpose and in the keeping of your promise.

Phenomenal teams link the WHY with WHO they have to be and therefore WHAT they need to do every day to reflect this commitment to the purpose.

THE WHO, THE HOW, THE WHAT, AND THE WHY

Phenomenal teams have total commitment to their brand and to working on and delivering their core behaviours every day.

They use these behaviours as drivers of performance, or as a springboard for action when challenged, as well as clues to where the gaps might be when they *don't* deliver on their promise.

In the above example, the challenge for the team was to agree on and build a set of behaviours. The whole team needed to become absolutely committed to those behaviours to ensure the delivery of their promise.

They needed to work on the WHO and the HOW in order to bring to life the WHY.

Not surprisingly, when we did a similar review with this organisation three months later, there was significantly more clarity regarding what the team stood for. It was aligned with their purpose, it was very clear who was committed to the delivery of the purpose and who wasn't, and, as a consequence, far more productive relationships had developed.

The business ran more quickly, performance improved, and delivery was quicker because the trust levels had been lifted.

THE PYRAMID PRINCIPLE

I was working in London with a global marketing team once, and over the course of a few months, we had built a team brand that everyone could recite, and some even had it as a screen saver!

The concern that the leader (let's call her Mary) faced was that the team – filled with young, bright, ambitious talent – would burn out. They were always really busy, always travelling, always working, and (importantly) always delivering.

Mary mentioned that they could recite *the purpose* and *the who* and *the what* when asked, and they could clearly articulate what the 'keep promise indicators' were. They could even tell you how they were progressing against them.

She did mention, though, that although the team now met far more regularly, meetings were rarely attended by all members because they were so busy.

When I asked how she would describe this team, Mary used words like 'stretched', 'busy', 'hardworking', 'deliverers', and 'a bit manic'. None of these was a part of the team brand.

Does this last point give us some clues as to where the problem might lie?

I challenged Mary's thinking with Figure 4.

Figure 4: The Pyramid Principle

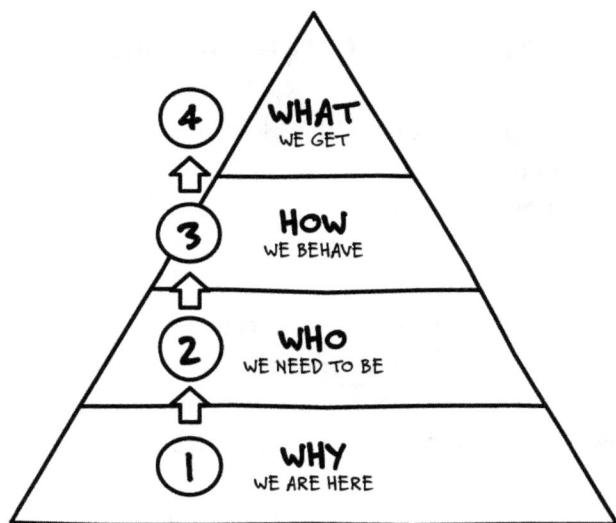

As mentioned before, the most stable structure humans have ever constructed is, arguably, the pyramid. I dare say the fact that ancient pyramids are still standing supports this claim!

One of the reasons for the strength of the pyramid is that its base is so stable.

Let's apply this principle to our work with developing phenomenal teams.

Phenomenal teams always have their purpose as the start of their action planning: 'Why are we here and who do we have to be?' rather than 'What do we need to get, and, therefore what do we need to do?'

Teams who start with 'What do we need to get, and, therefore, what do we need to do?' actually invert the pyramid. Their focus and all of their energy is committed to actions, without any reflection on who they need to be or who they are becoming. Who they need to be is given very little consideration because they are so caught up in the getting and doing.

Upon reflection, Mary could see where the problem lay. With the best intentions, the team had become so focused on getting what they needed to get and the 'doing' associated with that, that they had become a team far removed from their agreement as to why they were there, who the needed to be, and how they were to behave.

They had become a tired, busy, stretched team – in no way the aspirational team they had agreed to be. This was because 'effort' and 'doing' and 'getting' had become their focus. They were not focused on *being*.

Have you ever noticed that your team has become a little detached from how you want them to be seen?

To prevent this from happening, simply ask your team: 'If we lived our team brand 100 per cent of the time, what would we get?', and then list the two to three key outcomes for each behaviour.

In all my experience, the answer to this question often surfaces desired outcomes far beyond those that the team had been furiously chasing.

BUILD BEHAVIOURS

So how do we build the new behaviours that the team needs to be *committed* to?

In a similar way to how we built the team's purpose, the key to agreeing to *who* it has to be and therefore *what* it has to do starts with asking the questions that need to be answered, not avoiding or dismissing them.

Equally, just as the purpose has the most impact and will continually stretch your team when it is truly aspirational, this aspect of team development often has the most sustained impact when some of the agreed behaviours are aspirational, too.

So how do we do this?

1. COMPLETE A BEHAVIOURAL TEAM AUDIT
This exercise gives your team a quick behavioural audit of where they are at, and will identify some elements that cannot be

lost as the team grows. Equally, it will identify the areas that need to be addressed.

I would ask you to reflect on these questions from your own perspective first, then ask your team for their responses so that you can debate, reflect on, and discuss the answers:

- How would we describe ourselves?
- How would others in the organisation describe us?
- What words would they use?
- How do we need to be described if we are to deliver on our purpose?
- Is there a gap between who we need to be and how we are seen?
- What would others in the business see us do that reflects our strengths? (Make sure at this point that you are describing behaviours, not just grabbing words.)
- Which behaviours do we reward that add value to this team?
- Which behaviours do we reward that do not have any impact (or worse, may have a negative impact) on the delivery of our purpose?
- Which behaviours do we tolerate that hurt this team or will put our promise at risk?

2. IDENTIFY YOUR TEAM BRAND

Note that the responses to the first set of questions can often serve as a guide to the responses to the next set of questions.

The set of questions for your next conversation are:

- How do we need to be described if we are to keep our promise?

- Which of these behaviours are already evident?
- Which behaviours are missing?
- Which of our existing behaviours are adding value (and may come relatively easily to us) do we need to keep and, in fact, build on?
- Which behaviours do we need to stretch into? These tend to be behaviours that add real value but are only done now and then or when the conditions are right.
- Which behaviours are in our power zone? These are behaviours that would really accelerate our delivery and also ensure we no longer tolerate non-productive behaviours.

Once you have gathered, scribbled up, Post-it Noted, whiteboarded, or flip-charted, and shared all of these responses, the fun starts. You now have enough raw material to start building the day-to-day contributors to your purpose: *the how* and *the what*.

It is this team brand that you will not only agree on but agree to be committed to.

What you now need to be committed to is the next level of your development, sitting on the layer above trust.

Remember, phenomenal teams build from the bottom up. They start with *the why*, then *the who*, then *the how*, in order to get *what* they are driven to achieve.

As a consequence, the energy and effort are far more focused and deliberate and ensure clear alignment with how the team wants and needs to be seen.

Equally, team members' accountability (for both themselves and each other) is behaviourally focused, rather than solely outcome focused.

The team brand forms the basis for all our actions and decisions. Teams that enjoy enduring success have core values and a core purpose that remain unflinchingly fixed, whilst the strategies and practices endlessly adapt to what is becoming an increasingly disruptive world.

TIME OUT TO TALK ABOUT:

- Does your team have an agreed set of behaviours?

- Do you test each other's commitment to those behaviours regularly?

- Can you link these behaviours to your team's purpose?

- How often do you use an agreed set of behaviours as your starting point for reward, recognition, challenging, or action planning?

- Are these behaviours a mix of what you currently do well, what you could stretch into, and what you could adopt that would genuinely transform you?

- Do you ever ask an external group or groups for feed-back on what they are seeing from your team?

- Do you think your team is very clear on *why* they are, *who* they need to be, and *what* they need to do?

- Do you find your team consumed with 'busy-ness' and 'doing' at the expense of 'being'?

- Does your team always do what it says it is going to do?

CHAPTER FIVE

BUILD CREDIBILITY

f I were to ask you, and then your team members, to clearly articulate in twenty-five words or fewer what the team's strategy for growth or performance is, and to then list the top five strategic or operational imperatives, could you? And, importantly, would everyone say the same thing?

Equally, if I were to ask you and your team members what *collective success* or *high performance* looked like, would everyone say the same thing?

Now, I ask you to please be kind to yourself if you are unsure or answered 'no' to these questions!

David J. Collis, writing in the *Harvard Business Review*, observed that, in an astonishing number of organisations, senior executives, frontline employees, and everybody in between are frustrated, because there is a lack of clarity regarding the growth strategy and no clear plan exists to execute it. Consequently, leaders are mystified when initiatives fail to get implemented and projects are not delivered on time.

The reason I ask these questions is to set the scene for the next stage of our adventure. I have worked with a number of teams that get really excited about having clarity of purpose and having an agreed set of behaviours that they can hold each other accountable to, and yet, they are still not able to articulate the strategic priorities, agree on what the 'main thing' is, or whether they are really executing or performing.

> *Your team's strategy and the accompanying processes and action plans – all linked to the team's purpose – form the basis of your team credibility.*

Without it, the team, or more specifically the team members, get very lost and 'busy' (all with good intentions) pursuing lots of individual and separate tasks that may or may not be linked, integrated, or in any way adding value to the team's promise.

In sport, this is like having a group of players trying really hard every week to be brave and focused, eating all the right foods, and doing all the right preparation, but not being able to run, catch, or have any understanding of the game plan – if they even have one!

So, I want you to feel comfortable challenging the notion that commitment to your agreed behaviours – your culture – is in some way more important, or should take precedence over, establishing and maintaining *credibility*.

CULTURE VERSUS CREDIBILITY

'Culture eats strategy for breakfast', a phrase coined by Peter Drucker and given substantial attention by former Ford CEO Mark Fields, has often been the mantra when building high-performance teams.

I have witnessed, however, that, in the wrong hands, this notion almost gives leaders permission to spend all their attention on ensuring the cultural imperatives are being evidenced, with little or no attention to execution or performance.

My view, based on a number of years of having to work through this with teams, is that without strategy, culture will be very hungry when it pulls its chair up to the breakfast table and realises that there is nothing to eat!

Disconnecting the two will really put the performance of your team at risk.

It is almost as simple as asking yourself and your team: 'What would give this team credibility in terms of delivering on our purpose?'

A strategy for growth will certainly be one of the key elements.

Credibility – or what gives teams credibility – needs to be absolutely aligned with your commitments to your promise and behaviours, or culture.

Our next phase then ensures that we have answers to such questions as:

- Where are we going to play?
- How are we going to win?
- What skills or capabilities are needed to execute our strategy?
- How do we measure performance?
- Are we structured for growth?
- Are our processes good enough?
- Do we have clarity on the plan and do all of these aspects connect clearly to our purpose?

Make no mistake – phenomenal teams execute and deliver and they use their purpose as the test of that delivery. What the commitment to the purpose and that core set of behaviours enables is the long-term sustainability of that delivery or execution – and not at the expense of team engagement or growth, and not by risking talent burnout.

THE ART AND THE SCIENCE OF CREDIBILITY

Let me share with you a story about an organisation I once worked with.

The organisation in question was a small, boutique business in the technology space, which had been earning comfortable profits for some time and was very well regarded in its broader industry.

As the industry started to rapidly move in a far more market-driven and technology-enabled direction, one or two of the senior executives realised that they were positioned well to take advantage of these trends *if* they could accelerate a move out of their current comfort zone.

Initially, it seemed cultural change was what was needed. They needed to *become* a different team if they were to take advantage of the momentum within the industry and grow accordingly. As already mentioned, the reality of wanting to *become* a different team means creating an environment in which a different set of behaviours are rewarded.

The end game for the senior executives at this company was to make the business as attractive as possible as an acquisition target for a 'bigger player'.

This cultural shift was indeed my starting point, and the CEO and I spent a solid amount of time working with what, at the time, was a small team of a dozen or so people. We worked on defining the team's purpose, clarifying its behaviours, creating safety, rewarding those who embraced change, having the less-than-comfortable conversations that were required, and generally re-aligning the whole business.

Toward the end of this process, though, it became clear that in order for the company to *really* grow, and therefore be in a strong and attractive position to potential buyers, it needed to also build a new and exciting growth strategy.

There was clear evidence that the team was starting to regularly exhibit the new behaviours and embrace the purpose, and that a more trusting, collaborative, and cohesive environment was taking hold. The frustration, however, was that the strategies and processes we were challenging or enhancing were not growing the business quickly enough.

So, the CEO and I, along with his senior management team, embarked on a series of strategic workshops with the purpose of developing a clear, focused, and highly accountable strategic plan.

As per the building of the team brand, this process took place in stages and actions were continually reviewed, sometimes involving the entire business, and at other times involving only the senior management team.

> *The outcome was a strategy with accompanying process changes, action plans, and key priorities, and a purpose and team brand that were continually integrated.*

If the growth of the business slowed down at any point, it was easy to stop and conduct a review, with the understanding that delivery was driven off the team brand. We could then identify if there was a breakdown in behavioural commitment somewhere, and whether it was the *behaviour* that needed attention, rather than just the action plan.

What was the longer-term outcome from this continual focus

on the linking of commitment to the team brand with credibility? And of the use of *the purpose* as the springboard for the building of strategic initiatives?

The key, from my perspective, was that we now had an organisation delivering on all of their behavioural (and therefore cultural) commitments, while at the same time establishing significant credibility in the industry as an innovative, performance-based, and growth-focused business.

By the way, the owners of the business were eventually approached by that 'major player' and experienced an outcome far beyond what they initially expected!

So, what does all this mean?

Just as we are bringing together the art and science of building that phenomenal team, there is also an art and a science to building credibility with your team.

The *art* elements are those that require a degree of work from the team on the dynamics going on within its structure. Dare I say, this relies, to a very large degree, on how much effort has been made to build trust within the team, or, in the case of influence, trust with others external to the team.

The quality of the conversations, and the value the team puts on building trust will be a real determinant of the quality and reality of what is experienced here.

The *science* aspects, on the other hand, tend to be a little more clinical, and enable you as the leader to have, as a minimum, a well-managed business.

To be clear, phenomenal teams are managed well. However, teams that give an unbalanced amount of emphasis and energy to the science tend to be 'good' because their currency is based on effort and delivery.

Without the art, though, you may not maximise the talent within your team, and hence could put at risk the ongoing delivery – and credibility – of your team.

You need both art and science.

THE ART OF BUILDING CREDIBILITY

The art of building credibility is driven principally by alignment, balance, and influence, as shown in Table 3:

Table 3: The Art of Building Credibility

THE KEY ELEMENT	EXAMPLES OF WHAT IT MAY LOOK LIKE
The team is **aligned**.	• The team meets regularly and engages in productive, real conversations around the important strategic issues that connect to the team purpose. • Team members hold one another accountable to commitments and behaviours and celebrate successes. • The team promise and agreed behaviours are known by all team members. • All praise, development, and corrective actions and conversations relate to the agreed behaviours.
The team is **balanced**.	• The team has the right specialist skills and experience. • The team feels empowered to make decisions and does so. • The hierarchical leader allows real conversations to happen and doesn't feel the need to direct all meetings. • Ownership and accountabilities are clear.
The team has **influence**.	• Team members are skilled at understanding the needs of others (internally and externally) as well as their differences, priorities, and styles, and have an effective feedback process that drives improvements in trust.

THE SCIENCE OF BUILDING CREDIBILITY

The science of building credibility is principally driven by clarity, accountability and delivery, as shown in Table 4.

Before we go on, reflect on both the art and science of building your team's credibility.

What I have found to be a useful, reflective challenge at this point is to rate your team on the key elements by a simple rating, from one to three, on each of the six major elements: three for *the art* and three for *the science*:

- A score of 3 suggests you have the element in place and refer to it all the time.
- A score of 2 suggests you refer to and use the element some of the time.
- A score of 1 suggests you don't have this element in place, or you never refer to or use it.

For example, what would you rate your team for *alignment* (*art*) given the description of this element in Table 3? Or for *accountability* (*science*) given its description in Table 4?

I have found that the value in this exercise is twofold. First, it highlights which of the two – art or science – your team drifts to or prefers to operate in. Second, it highlights where your team's future growth might lie.

Table 4: The Science of Building Credibility

THE KEY ELEMENT	EXAMPLES OF WHAT IT MAY LOOK LIKE
The team has **clarity**.	• The team has a leader who is responsible for team performance, communication, and ownership. • The purpose of the team and the team brand are clearly defined and documented. • Everyone in the team is aligned with the number one thing that needs to be achieved this quarter or this year. • Ownership and accountabilities are clear. • The team members leave meetings with clear actions and specific agreements regarding decisions. • The key deliverables owned by the team are defined, agreed, and visible to all.
The team is highly **accountable**.	• The key delivery metrics are agreed and visible to all (both internally and externally). • The critical numbers, as they relate to the KPIs, are identified as well as the key priorities that support them. • Each team member has a critical number that aligns with the broader one. • The team is capturing feedback and reporting on KPIs is visible and used as real conversation starters to improve delivery levels.
The team is committed to **delivery**.	• The team has the necessary tools and processes in place, and they are well designed and optimised toward the delivery of the agreed KPIs. • Team members are aware of the progress each week toward the critical numbers and scoreboards that show this progress are displayed everywhere. • When delivery metrics slip, the team takes the time to address the issues.

Once you have your score, I have found it a fascinating exercise for the leader to ask the team members for their score without revealing his or her own!

It is not unusual for the leader of the team to suggest that they and the team members are very clear on what the growth strategy is and that they are able to articulate it. Unfortunately, the leader often assumes that the rest of the team agrees with his or her perspective when, in fact, their perspectives are far from aligned!

It is only by cross-checking these scores, and directly asking what the team believes are the top three or four strategic imperatives, that the leader can get a real sense of where the team is at, and whether, in fact, members are connecting their own initiatives and actions with the strategy and, hence, the purpose.

TIME OUT TO TALK ABOUT:

- How often are you using your team's purpose as the starting point for strategy-building conversations?

- Can you articulate your team's strategy for growth in twenty-five words or fewer?

- Can the rest of your team do the same?

- Can you clearly link your strategy with the delivery of your purpose?

- Are your available resources focused on the delivery of your promise?

- Does your action list add value to, and amplify, your promise?

- What score would you give your team for *the art* of building credibility?

- What score would you give your team for *the science* of building credibility?

- What score do other team members give along these dimensions?

- Where are the existing gaps in terms of your team's credibility?

CHAPTER SIX

HAVE REAL
CONVERSATIONS

would like to share a frustration I experienced during one of my early roles in my corporate career.

In this instance, the senior directors of a communications organisation I was working for felt that significant gains could be realised if we were to launch a business-to-business (B2B) business. This was their view even though the space was dominated by one major player with a long history in the market and strong client penetration in terms of product offering and processes.

The research did suggest, though, that customer satisfaction was generally quite low with this supplier, and that customers would change if there was a suitable alternative.

As part of our B2B launch, I was handed the opportunity to take the reins of a team that was attempting to penetrate, relative to the target segment, the biggest market in Australia.

Now, the team that I inherited had not been delivering and demonstrated mixed levels of performance.

My first major initiative was to get the sales teams and their managers to present their sales plans to me, which is where the frustrations started!

What do you think was at the heart of these frustrations?

Let's make a quick list of the reasons the sales teams gave for their inconsistent performance:

- 'The marketing team doesn't support us.'
- 'It takes too long for the accounts team to process changes.'
- 'We don't get access to the same products as our competitor.'
- 'Our competitor makes it too hard for the customer to move to us.'
- 'Our branding isn't strong enough.'
- 'When we do get the customer to agree, it takes too long for them to get their new bill.'

Have you ever heard something similar?

What I realised was that the team was externalising their performance. They were really happy talking about all of the external reasons why they were not performing well and could have talked about these external forces all day.

But what did they *really* need to talk about?

After their sales presentations, it became apparent that their sales plans were not good enough and they were not prepared to do the hard work to get in front of the customer.

In short, neither their credibility nor their commitment was good enough, but no one was prepared to talk about that.

The sales teams had been allowed to drift into, and stay in, the outside world, skirting around any action. The members of the team were happy to blame marketing, complain about the competition, and defend their own efforts.

What was needed were questions such as:

- 'What actions are you going to take?'
- 'What is stopping you from following up on that potential customer?'
- 'What could you do differently next time you get that response from another prospect?'

It was time to get real and take real action, which meant having real conversations!

BLAME, COMPLAIN OR DEFEND?

How many meetings have you sat in and asked yourself: 'Is anyone going to talk about that elephant sitting in the corner, or are we just going to blame, complain, or defend until it's time for our next meeting?'

How often have you sat in meetings and spent the whole meeting listening to people blaming, complaining, or defending?

How many meetings have you sat in to discuss performance delivery and listened to all the external reasons for not delivering and thought: 'When is someone going to talk about the plan we agreed to not being good enough, or our leadership not being good enough, or our skills not being good enough, or that person in our team who is selfish and self-serving?'

Or, what about those meetings where you have to review staff engagement, and you keep asking yourself: 'When are we going to push through all of these external reasons for poor engagement and focus on the fact that we are having high turnover because we are tolerating some very ordinary behaviour from each other that is forcing our talent to look elsewhere?'

When are we going to face the fact that talent leaves their leader?

What we are doing in all of these scenarios, my own included (and believe me, they are common) is shown in Figure 5.

What is missing is the focus on what we *really* need to talk about and do!

It is these real conversations that bring all the work done on building commitment and credibility to life.

Figure 5: Blame, Complain or Defend

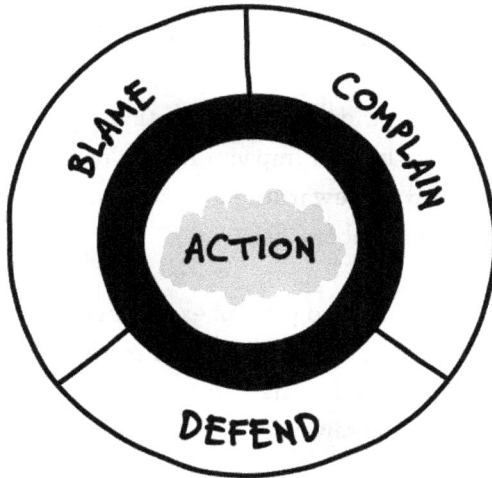

GET REAL

I deliberately use the term 'real conversation' for two reasons.

First, the *real* component ensures the focus is on: 'What do we really need to talk about right now if we want our performance to improve?' Or equally powerful: 'What do I really need to understand right now about what stage this person is at, or what stage my team is at?'

The conversation doesn't need to be 'hard' or 'difficult' or 'tough' or 'fierce', or any other negative adjective you might use that frames it as something it need not be. Describing the conversation in a negative way may create a mindset that could lead you to behave in a way that reflects your self-talk about the conversation. Your negative mindset surrounding the conversation may well result in a negative conversation, or even create such a negative emotion around it that you do whatever you can to avoid the conversation entirely.

Equally important, though, is the fact that the conversations that will have the biggest impact on your team's growth will be those focused on rewarding and recognising some great changes in team members' behaviour.

From my observations and years of experience across a number of fields, people are far more prepared to change behaviours if they are recognised for the effort. In simple terms, people repeat what they are rewarded for.

The second component of the phrase is the *conversation* element.

What is the primary characteristic of a conversation? That's right – a conversation goes both ways, and so it is important we separate the notion of 'feedback' from the real conversation.

> *Real conversations, which by definition go both ways, are very much focused on asking questions that seek to understand rather than dictating what needs to change.*

We run the risk that feedback, without the deliberate effort of seeking to understand, could be seen simply as your opinion.

Let's explore this a little further.

FROM 'I TELL' ...

It is not unusual for a leader to tell me they have just had a real conversation, when in fact they have simply undertaken a one directional stop-start-keep type of feedback exchange.

While I acknowledge that many successful organisations employ this type of framework, it is my observation that, in a number of these organisations, when feedback is mentioned, a troubling level of anxiety is evidenced. It runs the risk of being seen as a compliance tool.

Direct, one-way feedback is a very directive leadership style. Very much in the 'I tell, you do' mode.

There are moments when this style of leadership is appropriate, particularly when an issue is really urgent. But we must also seek to understand why somebody drifts into non-productive behaviour, or how a person learnt a certain skill so that they can help others, or why we only see that great behaviour in certain situations. If we, as leaders, don't do this, we are missing an opportunity to build trust, safety, and engagement.

Real conversations allow genuine, ongoing engagement of team members and provide teams with the opportunity to uncover, and own, the *real* issues affecting performance.

It is *now* that the investment in the building of meaningful working relationships, and therefore trust, will have the biggest impact.

What you are prepared to talk about, or feel safe talking about, when you come together to discuss performance will determine how quickly you grow. The real conversations are the accelerators of performance.

... TO 'HELP ME UNDERSTAND'

The key, then, lies in the need for us to move from a *telling* mode to an environment focused on *seeking* to understand, and linking the building of trust to the focus on *talking about the truth*.

At the heart of real conversations is seeking the answer to: 'What is the truth about us right now?'

The realisation and embracing of real conversations are based on a continual focus on the link between trust and the accompanying safety to talk about the truth.

Real conversations may well be initiated as follows:

- 'Help me understand what has happened here,'; or
- 'What role are we playing in where the team is at right now?'; or even
- 'Who in this team is really impacting the team's performance right now?'

And then move on to:

- 'What is the solution right now?' and
- 'What needs to change in this team for us to continue to improve?'

Conversations like this will ensure the focus is on the team, or even on the team members, and you are inviting others into the discussion, thereby providing an opportunity to really talk about what is happening.

> *Phenomenal teams are driven by real conversations. They seek to understand, they resolve issues quickly, they adjust quickly, they build more leaders quickly, they deliver more quickly, and, ultimately, they perform better.*

There is no need for a Plan B with the phenomenal team, as it is continually reviewing and adjusting Plan A!

SPACE FOR GROWTH

Phenomenal teams accept that it is the creation of an environment that enables the balanced bringing together of trust, truth, and talk that provides the space in which to have real conversations.

Let's examine three key observations I have witnessed when teams miss the opportunity to bring trust, talk, and truth together.

OBSERVATION ONE

The team assumes it has relatively high levels of trust, but while members do catch up to talk, they never really address the truth about their performance.

This team runs the risk of very quickly becoming that *fake* team identified in Table 1: Team Value Ladder from Chapter 2.

The safe place that fake teams go to when talking about performance is external. There is always an external reason for the team not performing – whether it be the competitors, the marketing department (or sales department if you are the marketing department!), or the referee, or whoever else you would love to complain about.

What's missing?

What's missing is a focus on the real conversation that needs to be had about performance. A question as simple as 'What could we actually do better?' may trigger a realisation that the team is actually playing a key role in its current level of performance. Keep in mind, though, that you may not be having this conversation because you have overestimated the level of trust.

OBSERVATION TWO

When teams bypass the building of trust and go straight into talking about the truth, this is a high-risk strategy. It presents itself through the observable, typically high-anxiety state of *fear*.

This is quite observable when broken down into the fight, flight, or freeze responses.

The group may push back and get aggressive or defensive, simply avoid the conversation, or just do nothing for fear of being wrong.

Giving stop-start-keep type feedback when trust levels are low or questionable is a classic trap that many well-intentioned leaders fall into.

What's missing?

What's missing is a safe, high-trust environment. In fact, that could well be the real conversation the leader needs to have with themself: 'What is needed right now for team members to feel safe talking about the truth?' Or equally powerfully: 'How am I contributing to this team not feeling safe?'

OBSERVATION THREE

Now, the third scenario is an equally interesting one, as it typically happens when the team is going well. It is not unusual for me to hear language like: 'We are winning, so we don't really need to catch up and review,' or 'We are so busy getting things done right now we don't have the time.'

It may not be long, though, before this team experiences a *WOA Moment* – that is, a *width of acceptance* moment.

These moments occur when the team is starting to ignore what, at the time, seems like insignificant slips in standards, until these slips build up to a significant moment. This is the moment when the team asks itself: 'Woa(h), when did we start accepting *this*?'

Corporate and sporting history is littered with these WOA moments that have been the culmination or compound effect of walking past slips in standards because we're 'too busy', or more worryingly 'because we're winning'.

A team that continually misses deadlines may well have started out as the team (and the leader) that started accepting that 'a day late every now and then is okay'.

What's missing?
What's missing is truly valuing the time it takes to have the real conversation. A question that could start some real conversations is: 'Have we ignored anything lately that we should have addressed?'

Without the balanced bringing together of trust, truth, and talk, genuine growth opportunities can be missed.

MOVING THE ELEPHANT OUT

I once worked with a senior leadership team in the finance sector, and we were having quite a strategic discussion on what would accelerate the business's growth. As you would expect, a number of the suggestions were all very technical and necessitated the head office spending money on product development, or on marketing campaigns, or on the customer relationship management system. Every now and then, they drifted into talking about the performance of areas of the business not represented in the room.

I was getting a sense that the team was starting to get very comfortable with externalising the conversation, and with avoiding any 'elephants'.

So, I stopped to summarise my observations and suggestions, and asked the group: 'What are you seeing from each other that is frustrating your growth?'

The silence was broken by a brave, recent addition to the team, who observed quite candidly that, 'One of the quick wins we could buy into is to stop hoarding clients, and allow others access so that we could introduce them to products and services that the key account manager doesn't know much about.'

You can imagine the initial response, can't you?

The group moved rather quickly from a very vociferous denial, to a degree of acceptance, to a much quieter realisation that it was true.

The leader then asked the question: 'Help me understand why you would possibly be denying other members of this team access to clients that we could be selling other services to?' Note how much more insightful and powerful it is to ask a question, rather than simply telling the team to stop doing it and start sharing.

As it turned out, after much discussion, they realised that the current reward system needed to be far more reflective of the efforts of the whole team, as a number of team members had become consumed with their own personal rewards.

A few things happened when the reward system was aligned off the back of this real conversation. The team grew the business significantly the next year and developed much deeper relationships with their clients, all with very little assistance from head office. And those that were driven by individual financial rewards soon drifted out of the organisation.

The other great outcome was that, because the leader had encouraged, rewarded, and recognised the bravery in initiating the real conversations, meetings became far more robust, strategic, and action based.

Kobe Bryant, in his book *The Mamba Mentality*, suggested that what separated great players from all-time-great players was their ability and willingness to self-assess, diagnose weaknesses, and turn those flaws in to strengths. It is no different with teams.

By bringing together trust, truth, and talk, your team will create genuine growth opportunities. These real conversations will accelerate your team's growth.

> *It is amazing how much space becomes available in a room once we get the elephant out of there!*

TIME OUT TO TALK ABOUT:

- When your team meets, is it a work-in-progress meeting? Or is the focus on 'What do we *really* need to talk about for us to grow and deliver on our purpose?'

- When your team meets to discuss *credibility* and *commitment*, do you hear the language of 'blame, complain, and defend'?

- Have you noticed some small things go unsaid or are tolerated because you are either 'too busy' or 'winning'?

- Do you stop as a team and reflect on who in the team makes a real effort to change and who does great work?

- Is feedback in your team a compliance tool or a genuine opportunity to seek to understand? Is it a real conversation or is it more 'I tell, you do'? Do you see team members get anxious with the notion of feedback?

- Do all your team members feel safe in challenging the way the team is currently operating?

PART THREE

BE IN IT TO WIN IT

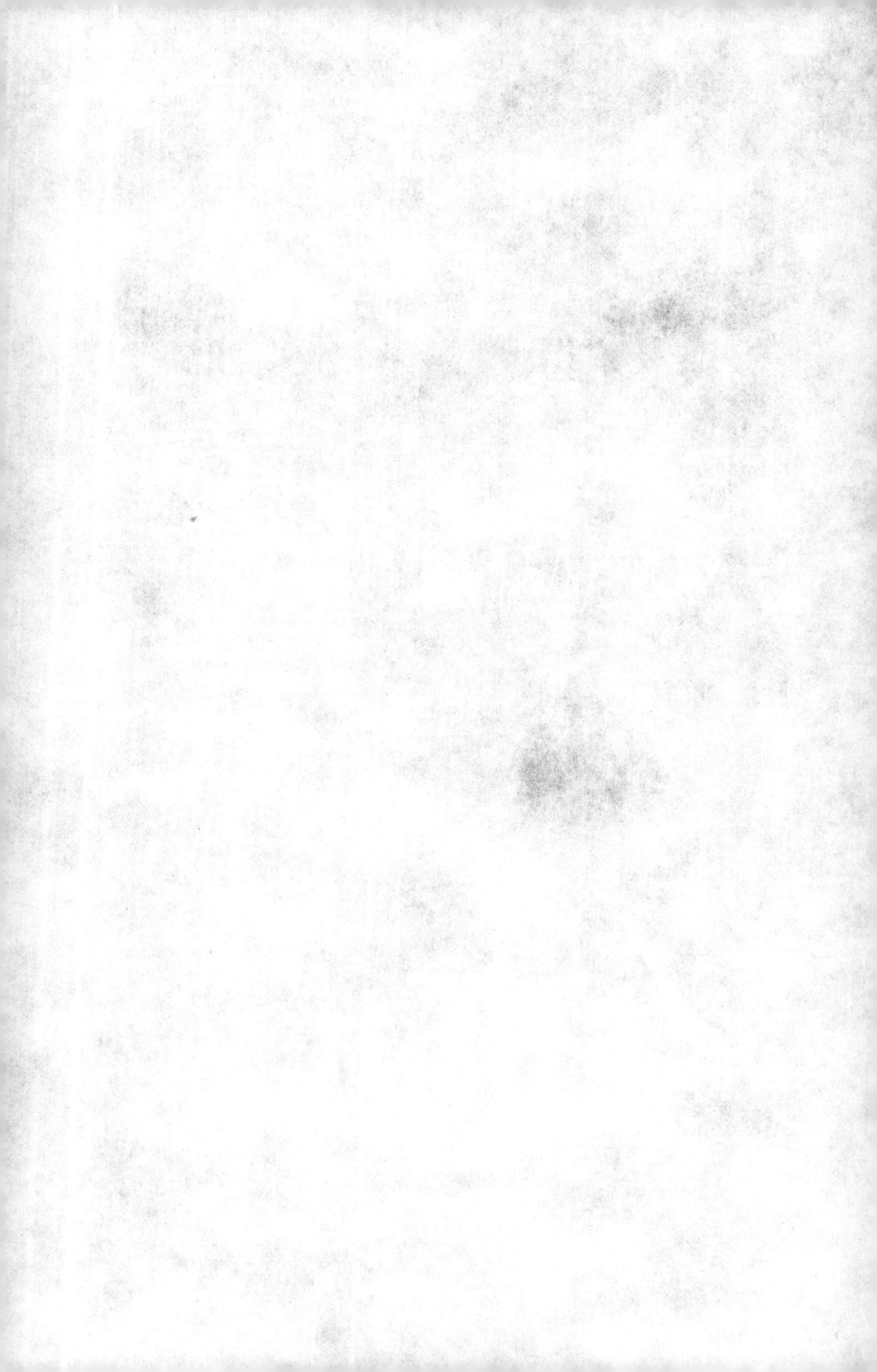

BE IN IT TO WIN IT

et me share a secret with you. I struggle with my weight and my fitness!

And don't worry, I have relied on all of the age-old excuses: travel, busy-ness, workload, work pressure, client pressure, family commitments, weather, timing ... have I missed anything?

When I reflect, the whole process goes a little like this ...

I think about it – particularly after catching myself in the mirror and then getting on the scales for the first time in a few weeks or months. I then talk about it – particularly to those close to me. I may even download a weekly diet from the internet, or join a gym, or sign up for the latest online weight control and fitness program.

After having this conversation a few times though, and after showing and telling my friends about the diet and fitness programs I have downloaded, what are my close friends looking for from me to test the earnestness of my commitment?

Yes – action! They want me to link my words to actions!

Now, once I have started doing something, what keeps me motivated? Of course, seeing the difference on the scales and feeling fresher and stronger will provide some internal motivation, but what potentially has the *most* impact?

Right – when *others* notice! When that person in the office or in one of my workshops actually tells me that they have noticed. From here, I get really excited and start to lock in those habits that I have been working so hard on. Let's face it, I want to get that recognition again!

In the final stage, my habits have just become who I am. They are part of my character and require little, if any, internal debate. I have come to realise, too, that this process never ends. There is never a point when I can say, 'So glad that is done, I am fit now!' For me to maintain whatever gains I have made, I must continue to work hard at those established habits.

Your team will undertake a very similar journey. The development of a phenomenal team is an ongoing process.

So, let's get into that now.

CHAPTER SEVEN

GET READY FOR THE LONG GAME

M y mother – a wonderful, pragmatic lady from the North of England – would often warn me that 'bad luck comes in threes'.

Well, unfortunately, when it comes to teams believing that the job is done after one moment of success, I have three very clear experiences.

Without going into detail, each team – all sporting teams – had initially felt that a 'cultural change was needed if they were to be successful'. The intent was admirable, and one that I felt could lay the foundation for sustained success for each of the respective teams.

With each team, we built an environment of trust, a team purpose, and a core set of behaviours and values. We then set about holding each other to account, and only rewarding and recognising those who lived out the agreed behaviours.

Not surprisingly, each team experienced improved success, and leaders started to emerge. These were signposts that suggested we were certainly on the right path – at least from my perspective.

In all three cases though, come the following season, I was presented with comments like 'I think we got what we needed,' or 'I think I can take it from here' or 'I think the leadership group can now drive this'.

Unfortunately, the ensuing result suggested otherwise. Each team in question failed to scale the heights previously reached with performances becoming inconsistent and below those from the previous season.

Let us compare that with a different conversation I was having at roughly the same time, with another head coach in a different, yet equally high-profile team, in a different code.

I had worked with this coach for a number of seasons, and the team had recently won the Premiership. This team prided itself on the culture that had been developed and the role it was playing in driving long-term success.

In fact, some of the mythology around the building of this team's culture transcended sport. It wasn't unusual for CEOs I met to aspire to build a culture similar to the one this team had.

This head coach was focused entirely on: 'How do we keep

getting better, because our competition are, and how do we ensure that our success and the culture that supports our drive for success is not only maintained, but grows?'

As a consequence, we built upon the foundations we'd put in place, to the point where this team played in two more Grand Finals and only missed playing finals once in the following ten years.

So, what was the key difference here, and what was my key learning that I think is worth sharing?

All four of the head coaches were extremely likeable, well credentialed, knowledgeable and respected, but it was the understanding and commitment to the notion that building a phenomenal team is an ongoing process that set the last head coach apart from the first three.

The head coaches of the first three teams had built good teams. They had their 'moment in the sun'. Whereas, the latter coach understood that good is only a starting point and was determined to use the winning of a Premiership as merely a signpost that they were heading in the right direction, not the sign that they had arrived at their destination.

Phenomenal teams are built to last. And that means your work is never done (although it does get easier).

The other significant point, which may well be worth pausing and thinking about, is that the absence of counterproductive or troublesome team members does not mean that you have now built a high-performance environment.

The coaches who felt that they had built the finished product had fallen into the view that, because members of the team no longer exhibited the counterproductive behaviours, they must have built a high-performance environment.

What is the learning, then, as we embark on our own adventure?

I suggest that we have an honest look at these critical questions when we embark on our quest:

- Am I just looking for a way to deal with those in the team whose behaviour is proving to be problematic?
- Am I genuinely committed to creating a high-performance environment in which occasional tension and conflict will be experienced – or an environment in which everyone 'behaves themselves' and 'gets on'?
- Am I prepared to take a long view of this process, or do I just need to get better quickly?

For it is my view that simply putting cultural or behavioural standards in place as a way to exit or isolate those causing the team to be somewhat slower or even mildly dysfunctional is too short-sighted an approach.

Building a high-performance environment is about sustained performance, not about building a team of well-behaved or compliant members.

Dealing with, or even eliminating counterproductive behaviours is a natural outcome of the process and creates the foundation for the creation of a high-performance environment, but it does not define one.

SUSTAINABLE SUCCESS

How many teams have you been in or led that have had a remarkable year, but struggled to maintain that performance the next year or the year after that? Or after a couple of the star performers have left, or after you have run out of energy?

Figure 6 gives us some clues as why this happens so often.

Figure 6: High-Performance Team Progress

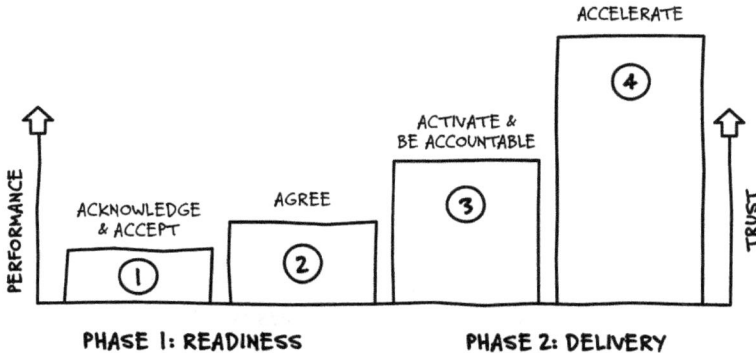

Stages 1 and 2 constitute the Readiness phase. Stages 3 and 4 reflect the Delivery (or Execution) phase.

Let's have a look at these stages in a little more detail.

STAGE 1: ACKNOWLEDGE (AND ACCEPT)

Any cultural change is, in essence, a change in behaviour. And when we ask teams to get better, this is what we are essentially looking for. But when we do this, the question 'Why?' will arise in the minds of some.

Now, in a number of instances, the answer could be quite obvious:

- We have missed budget three quarters in a row.
- Our last project was delivered late.
- The economic or technological environment has shifted.
- We have new owners and they have increased targets compared to last year's budget.
- Our competitors have caught up with us.

Whatever it is, it is essential that we be able to clearly articulate or demonstrate *the why*.

Now, understanding *the why* and being willing to change are not guaranteed!

Thus, the second crucial aspect here is the team's *acceptance* that they will need to change to address what could have an impact on future performance.

> *Being in the same team, yet expecting different results is a high-risk approach. In fact, it is an approach founded on hope and luck!*

STAGE 2: AGREE

Once we have moved the team toward accepting that they will need to be a different team and go about their work in a different way if expecting a different result, we need to *agree* on what, specifically (particularly in terms of behaviour) will need to change or be added.

It is accepted that some of the changes may also be around the credibility of the business or team. The strategy, structure or product development may all need to be addressed. However, once these changes are in place, it will be choices in behaviour that will drive success.

To reinforce the point, it is during this stage that trust and safety become so important.

As mentioned in earlier chapters, during this process we may well be asking the question: 'Which behaviours have we been tolerating within this team that will prevent us being that phenomenal team?' And equally impactful: 'And who from?'

Now, the answers to these types of questions are pivotal to building a set of 'go-forward' behaviours, and yet without high levels of trust and safety, we may miss out on getting to the *real* issues, as indeed these are the real conversations.

The key outcome here is agreement on what our team brand will be that will ensure we maximise the opportunities in the new world and deliver on our 'keep promise indicators'.

As mentioned, a number of teams quite happily get to *agreement*.

What we do every day, how committed we are to our agreement, and how we go about activating this agreement every day will now define us.

STAGE 3: ACTIVATE (AND BE ACCOUNTABLE)

Now, this is the part that really starts to drive success. How do we ensure that what we have just agreed to is actually embedded in the way we go about our business?

It is during this period that we hardwire the *plan, execute, review model* as part of our operating rhythm.

The team will build everything around the delivery on the purpose (or promise). Phenomenal teams are purpose driven.

Everything they do ensures the keeping of their promise.

The real conversations will ensure constant focus on rewarding and recognising the positive gains, or that we challenge ourselves when we slip.

The team will openly challenge behaviour that is not acceptable or that slows down performance, while at the same time rewarding and recognising those who are clearly having a positive impact.

Feedback will be a mix of formal and informal.

Issues will be dealt with quickly. The truth will be embraced, and the actions aligned accordingly.

This is when that FAAST team starts to emerge.

We are no longer tolerating the language of victims – whether it be blame, complain, or defend. It is during this period that we start to create and develop Action Heroes!

STAGE 4: ACCELERATE

This stage gives you the opportunity to share the energy workload. It is during this phase that other leaders around you start to pick up the mantle, and you start to take comfort in the impact of the legacy you are building.

It is also at this point that a good number of your team realise and embrace what you have defined in your team brand, and the ensuing behaviours you reward and recognise define what leadership looks like in this team.

The conversations at this exciting stage start to focus on issues such as:

- Who is the next wave of leaders within this team?
- Where else could we now replicate this process?
- Who is there outside of this team that we should start developing?

- Are all team members starting to develop their own success?
- What can we do to accelerate the performance of this team or the development of those emerging leaders?
- How can we stretch them?
- How can we start recruiting against our team brand so that we already have potential leaders when they start?

The observation, and potential obsession that phenomenal teams are led by many, underpins and becomes a major focus at this stage.

> *This obsession with identifying the next wave of leaders before the current leaders have left is the biggest single difference between a great team and a phenomenal team.*

So how can you tell what stage you are in right now?

A couple of simple questions may help:

- **What do you use as starting points for addressing any challenges you may have in this team?** Assuming that team members can articulate the purpose and agreed behaviours without prompting (therein may lie the first test!), ask yourself as the leader whether, in fact, you refer to the purpose and aligned behaviours that you have committed to when starting conversations around performance. If you're not, you are still in the agreement stage.

- **What are we using to determine what high performance looks like?** What will make a team member highly capable will be the combination of skill and delivery on the key behaviours. If you are just looking at skill, then you are simply using competence as the measure.

How often have you witnessed team members being rewarded, in any number of ways, despite knowing that they are not living the agreed behaviours?

Again, if this is happening then you have simply agreed to a set of behaviours without using them to drive or reward performance

FROM READINESS TO DELIVERY

The *readiness phase* of the High-Performance Team Progress in Figure 6 – the stages involving *acknowledgment* and *agreement* – is the easier of the two phases to achieve. A number of factors can indicate that you are in this phase: posters on the wall displaying organisational or team values, or highlighted pages in the HR induction books, are examples of *readiness*.

Many teams get to this phase, and I am sure you have been at offsites where a day (or multiple days) was dedicated to agreement about the team's or the organisation's values, only to never hear about them again until yearly appraisal time! The team has determined their agreed purpose, their agreed behaviours, and their agreed team brand. In fact, it would be hard to miss these as they are plastered all over the walls in the office, on mouse pads, and on coffee cups.

In fairness, these 'ready' teams may see a short-term improvement in their performance, and the trust levels may improve to some degree, as some people in the team are starting to feel safe to challenge and ask some great questions.

From my experience, the best we can hope for with teams that just 'get ready' is that they will be a good team. They will have the occasional great moment that gets the team really excited and fuels hope for the future, but will then get busy and become consumed with just getting things done in order to 'get what we want'.

> *It is the commitment to the delivery phase that ensures movement from good to great to phenomenal.*

The first thing we need to appreciate, and take comfort in, is that there is a structure and a process to that movement.

Phenomenal teams – in fact, even good and great teams – have got to where they are with structure and discipline, and equally an appreciation that teams need to move through particular phases in order to achieve that phenomenal status.

To simply get agreement on your team brand and then look to accelerate the growth of others within the organisation runs the risk of missing the opportunity to build a real foundation within your own team.

Your own team needs to be progressing through this process before you can ask others to join in.

A simple example of this is when a senior leadership team finally gets clarity on their purpose and behaviours, and then immediately starts to look at implementing or initiating a sort of emerging-leaders-type program or rolling the process through a number of teams in an effort to accelerate the growth before the leadership team has genuinely progressed itself.

These are admirable initiatives, without doubt, and full of great intentions, but they are potentially flawed if the senior leadership team is still trying to embed its brand and behaviours itself.

Obviously, it is the second phase (the *delivery phase*) that will define your team's performance and, therefore, its brand.

The phases focusing on the activation of these values and the acceleration of them throughout the team will drive ongoing performance.

WHAT DOES LEADERSHIP LOOK LIKE?

Broadly speaking, and most significantly if you are the designated senior leadership team, the way your team now operates is the single biggest definer of 'what leadership looks like around here'.

How often have you observed teams that, despite having had many years of success, go flat once the leader or key team members leave?

Now – let's get back to my original challenge.

Building a phenomenal team will need you to be on this for the long haul and to accept that this team will not be built in a day, but will be built daily!

> *Building that phenomenal team takes time, and there may well be times when you think you are the only one who cares about it. But I am asking you to commit to this adventure.*

As a community, we need more phenomenal teams. Your organisation needs more phenomenal teams, and we need you to become that legendary leader of a phenomenal team.

As you move through the discipline, structure, and support needed throughout the development of these stages, you *will* start to build more leaders. Your team's successes *will* become sustainable. Your team members *will* become more engaged. You *will* get to focus more on the high-impact strategic growth factors, and you *will* build a legacy that lasts.

> *Leadership WILL become your lifestyle choice!*

TIME OUT TO TALK ABOUT:

- Are you in this for the long game?

- Are you all in agreement with the team brand? Is it visible and can team members articulate it quickly when asked?

- Is the team brand at the centre of every discussion concerning performance?

- Is it really clear to all how to 'behave your way into your team'?

- Is there also an understanding that you could 'behave your way *out* of the team'?

- Are team members held to account by each other?

- How quickly and how often are team members rewarded and recognised for living the behaviours?

- Do you recruit for your team against the agreed behaviours?

- What is being done to stretch and grow those team members in demonstrating the agreed behaviours?

- Have you and each team member identified a development plan for successors?

- How close is your team to being that phenomenal one that everyone wants to be in?

YOUR TEAM HEALTH CHECK

Get everyone on your team, including yourself, to fill out this health check individually. Your results should form the starting point for your next leadership team meeting.

Rate each of these key attributes. They are critical to understanding where your team might be at right now.

Where:

5 = We are exceptional at this
4 = We are really good at this, but every now and then we slip
3 = This happens in our team when the conditions are right
2 = This happens in our team every now and then
1 = This very rarely happens in our team

(By the way – no 'in betweens', for example, no 1.5s!)

ATTRIBUTE	IT LOOKS LIKE ...	1	2	3	4	5
TRUST	Members of the team trust one another and feel they can be genuinely vulnerable with each other.					
	Team members hold one another accountable to commitments and behaviours and celebrate team successes.					
	The team meets regularly and engages in productive, real conversations around important issues that impact on the delivery of the team purpose.					
	All team members feel safe having conversations with each other about performance and do not leave these conversations to senior members of the team.					
PURPOSE	Our purpose is agreed and can be clearly articulated by all team members.					

ATTRIBUTE	IT LOOKS LIKE ...	1	2	3	4	5
	Team members leave meetings with clear and agreed priorities and actions and specific agreements around decisions pertaining to the delivery of the purpose.					
	Our purpose significantly influences the strategic direction, actions, and priorities of this team.					
	Our purpose is on the agenda for every leadership meeting.					
COMMIT-MENT	Our team leader actively engages with, and creates opportunities for, team members to lead, and allows real conversations to happen without directing them.					
	In this team, ownership and accountabilities are clearly defined and each team member takes the opportunity to lead when required.					

ATTRIBUTE	IT LOOKS LIKE ...	1	2	3	4	5
	The behaviours that team members need to be committed to are agreed, clearly articulated, and used to drive delivery of the purpose.					
	This team pushes through *blame*, *complain*, *defend*, and looks to take action quickly.					
CREDIBILTY	Team members are skilled at understanding the needs of their 'customers' and have an effective feedback tool that drives improvement.					
	The strategy for driving, improving, and igniting the purpose is clear and can be clearly articulated by all in the team.					
	The team has the necessary tools and processes in place to deliver on the purpose, and these are well designed and are being optimised.					
	Success metrics connect directly to our purpose.					

Now, tally up your score for each of the attributes, and compare that score to the maximum score of twenty for that attribute to give you some potential areas to focus on and have *real* conversations about.

There is little benefit to calculating a grand total score out of eighty, as that doesn't really identify where the issues may lie. However, a score of twelve out of twenty for *trust* does clearly identify a starting point.

Just a word of support here: be kind to yourself. The fact that you are even doing this health check puts you ahead of most leaders.

I suspect that there are very few teams that would really rate a five for every area. (Just as I suspect that there would be few teams that would rate a one for every element.) I will add though, that phenomenal teams will rate *very* highly on all these attributes.

Equally, though, with that thought in mind, don't lose sight of what you may be doing well. There may be an area here that you and all your team members rate consistently high. Can I ask you to embrace that? Identify what you are doing to deliver on that and *keep doing it*!

Once you have completed this health check, simply reflect on the following question:

'What does this suggest that we REALLY need to act on and where is our opportunity for growth?'

WHAT NEXT?

As mentioned more than once throughout the book, your actions as a leader reflect what you value. Just by getting to the end of this book, it's clear that you value the building of a better team. So, well done and, most of all, thank you for coming on this journey with me!

You now may also be thinking, 'But where do I start? What is something simple I could do tomorrow to at least get my team thinking about how much better we could really be?'

Here are some ideas to start.

Get a sense of where your team is currently at by:
- completing your Team Health Check and using your results as the basis for your next leadership team meeting.

Build meaningful working relationships and start making some deposits into the trust ATM by:
- having conversations (beyond work) tomorrow with each of your team members to help you understand them a little more and build that environment of trust; and
- understanding what they expect from you and what they

need to feel valued, while at the same time making sure they understand what you expect from them.

Become more *purposeful* as a team by:

- sitting with your leadership team to confirm or agree on your purpose and what will be your promise back to your organisation. Agree on who you now need to be and what the core behaviours are that will define you.

Help your team build *credibility* by:

- putting your team's purpose or promise in the centre of a whiteboard, flipchart, or equivalent, and asking your team what they could do to ignite it, improve on it, investigate with respect to it, or implement it in order to give your leadership team credibility.

Have *real conversations* by:

- preferably once a month, but certainly once per quarter, making a team member your single focus for having real conversations about the leadership team's performance and that individual's performance relative to the agreed behaviours.

The reason I am asking you to start thinking about taking actions now is that I am hoping that another of the key messages you have picked up throughout this book is that building a phenomenal team is not about slogans on the wall, or charters, or guiding principles, or visible lists of below-the-line and above-the-line-behaviours, or the like.

Make no mistake, these are all great starting points, but they are simply that – starting points. Reading them, or being able to recite them, will not guarantee acting on them.

You need to be in this for the long game, and continually looking for ways to keep this process alive if you are going to be truly committed to the building of a phenomenal team.

Activating what you have agreed on is the key to this. Once you have built that environment of high trust, using your purpose and your agreed behaviours as conversation starters, recruitment tools, strategy starters, problem solvers, and reward platforms will all serve to bring your agreements to life.

And by creating and developing more leaders outside of your current leadership team, you will serve to accelerate your organisation's or team's ongoing performance.

So many aspiring leaders lose sight of the fact that team members are far more likely to remember how they *felt* being in your team than their daily task list.

Your legacy as a leader could well lie in your team members, when asked about their time in your team, simply replying, 'We all felt like leaders'!

Through these efforts, you will also start to build high performance that will endure.

LET'S CONNECT!

As mentioned at the outset, the building of a high-performance environment is very much an adventure. It will not happen simply because you decide to create an event that highlights the benefits, the challenges, or even the process.

You may be able to excite your team members about the growth possibilities for them all, should they embrace the creation of that Phenomenal Team at that particular event, but it will take a committed approach to getting it started.

So, with this in mind, there are a number of ways we could connect and start this wonderful adventure together.

My primary mode of delivery is the facilitation, through dedicated workshops, of the Stretch to Grow High Performance Team Program.

Typically, a team and that team's leader would see this as a twelve-month (six months minimum) process that would also be aligned with individual leadership development and mentoring.

Ideally, the starting point would be the leader and their direct reports.

Equally though, I often speak at conferences, workshops, or as part of a broader 'kick start' to a particular time of year. For example, speaking at sales kick-offs, senior team offsites, leadership development days, or strategic planning days can all provide opportunities to present the characteristics of, or spark an interest in, the creation of high-performance environments.

At a more intimate level, I do a good deal of one-on-one mentoring. It is not unusual for a leader to initially engage in a Stretch to Grow Mentoring Leadership Program that has a similar approach with a similarly aligned framework to the one experienced in this book, prior to commencing work with their team.

Now that you have read this book (again, thank you so much!), I would like to think it has at least triggered some thinking about you, your team, and how much potential you could unlock in your team. So, to that end – contact me. Our first catch-up coffee is on me!

Finally, at the very least, if you are just looking for the latest thinking on building Phenomenal Teams and your development as a leader, go to gariedooley.com and register for my newsletter.

The best way to get in touch directly? Just write to garie@gariedooley.com.

I cannot wait to hear about you and your team!

www.ingramcontent.com/pod-product-compliance
Lightning Source LLC
Chambersburg PA
CBHW071654210326
41597CB00017B/2210